THE METHODIST CHURCH IN AFRICA SINCE 1820

Authorship by
PIANAPUE KEPT EARLY, PH.D.

Foreword by
BISHOP DAVID GREAVES

Alabama-West Florida Conference
The United Methodist Church
Montgomery, Alabama

PACEM IN TERRIS PRESS

www.paceminterrispress.com

*Copyright © 2020 Pianapue Early
All rights reserved.*

*Under international intellectual property laws,
no part or the whole should be distributed for profit,
without prior approval from the author.*

ISBN 978-1-7330475-6-2

*Cover image Maletsunyane Falls in Lesotho
Shutterstock*

PACEM IN TERRIS PRESS
*is the publishing service of
the Pacem in Terris Ecological Initiative,
which is the core project of*

PAX ROMANA / CMICA-USA
*1025 Connecticut Avenue NW, Suite 1000,
Washington DC 20036
www.paceminterris.net*

ABOUT THE AUTHOR

PIANAPUE TK EARLY is an Elder in Full Connection in the Alabama – West Florida Conference, the United Methodist Church. He is Pastor of Theodore First UMC, Theodore, Alabama. He is originally from Liberia. Pianapue enjoys going in mission trips and playing football (soccer) during his spare time. He is married to Dr. Claudette L. Williams.

ACKNOWLEDGEMENTS

This work is possible because of God, the giver of life, liberation, love, and wisdom.

I am grateful to Bishop Greaves for his input in this project and his support of this work. I pray that the Church of the Alabama-West Florida Conference will continue the path of bringing people to God.

I am grateful for Dr. Joe Holland, who is a mentor and a colleague. His advice and suggestions are always helpful.

I acknowledge members of the Early, Gaye, Johnson, Sanders, and Weah Families of Liberia and the United States of America, for their continuous support and prayers. I am especially grateful to Mr. Ousley Natt Early, Sr., Minneapolis, Minnesota, who serves as an advisor in this and other projects.

And last, but certainly not the least, I always give credit to Claudette, my wife and friend/critic, for her support and hard work.

DEDICATION

This book honors all who helped Methodism grow in Africa

and

Honorable Wilmot Neekpo Howard, Sr.

of Pawtucket, Rhode Island,

a real child of God.

TABLE OF CONTENTS

Foreword, *by Bishop David Greaves*	1
Preface	5
1. Early Methodist Society in Africa Beginning in 1820	9
2. Methodist Missionary Bishops in Africa since 1856	27
3. Methodist Church in Africa: Overview since 1800	45
4. African Methodism & American Roots since 1800	57
5. Methodist Indigenous Bishops in Africa since 1964	73
6. Methodist Mission Targets & Bassa People since 1900	79
7. Conclusion	97
Appendix: List of Methodist Bishops who served in Africa	101
Bibliography	103
Other Books from Pacem in Terris Press	109

FOREWORD

Bishop David Greaves

As a fourth generation Methodist and part of the United Methodist Church for over 50 years, I have always been intrigued by people's personal history and church history.

My great grandfather owned a laundry truck pulled by a horse in the town where I grew up. I never met him, but he paved the way for my family to join the Methodist Church. My grandfather owned an auto parts store in town where he was involved in county politics and the Methodist Church. He witnessed the United States Methodist merger consisting of the Methodist Church North and South in 1939.

Yet segregation still existed among black and white people, as African American Methodists were relegated to a Central jurisdiction. This continued until 1968, when the Methodist Church, the United Brethren Church, and the Central Jurisdiction came together to form the United Methodist Church.

Because of my great-grandfather and grandfather, my father grew up in the church now known as The United Methodist Church. He has been a member of the church for 80 years; the same church where I was raised. He retired as a vice president for a large sporting-goods manufacturer and influenced as a young adult what I thought would be my career in sports management.

However, God had a different idea and I answered the call to ordained ministry. I had no idea where the journey would take me. Four generations later, I am serving as a Bishop in the United Methodist Church.

Our history is important. It reminds us of our heritage and home. We even might find that parts of our history are shameful or hurtful. Yet I am reminded that if we do not talk about our history, we miss out on some of the meaningful parts of who we have become. It also reminds us that there are parts of our history; we do not wish to repeat.

My journey as a United Methodist has led me to be assigned as the resident bishop of the Alabama-West Florida Conference. I am blessed to serve alongside one of my pastors, Dr. Pianapue TK Early. We fondly call him, "PK".

Pianapue Early's book gives a concise history of the first settlers from Europe and other countries along with the Methodist pastors and bishops to Africa. He brings out the diversity around Christianity in Africa and how the Methodist movement impacted the mission of Christ.

Just as the missionary movement in America was vital to our nation's formation, the Methodist missionaries to Africa created a movement that continues to this day, growing the Christian Church all over the continent of Africa. It is African leaders who are now giving leadership to this vital and growing movement.

There is part of the United Methodist history in Africa that was hurtful, as colonialism was in the mix. Yet, the greatest days of the church in Africa are in front of it.

We in America have much to learn from reading this history. I am grateful for Dr. Early writing this book and placing it before us.

Our history tells a lot about us. You will be blessed as you read about the United Methodist history in Africa explained in this book. What a wonderful gift from Pianapue Early this piece is.

DAVID W. GRAVES

Resident Bishop of the Alabama-West Florida Conference
United Methodist Church

PREFACE

IN discussing Methodism in Africa, it is important to disclose that, as presented in this work, Methodism includes the forerunners of the current United Methodist Church, from which the African Methodist Episcopal Church; the African American Episcopal Zion Church; the Christian Methodist Church, and now the current United Methodist Church, which was formally established in 1968. The discussion focuses on the current United Methodist Church efforts in Africa with its forerunners, but a discussion in which we cannot ignore other Methodist bodies that made contributions to the growth of the Methodism, as a Christian denomination.

In January 2020, African Methodism became 200-years old, from the time when the first Methodist settlers with African roots arrived in today's Liberia in January of 1820.[1] Not long after, in 1847, the new country of Liberia declared its independence.

---

[1] In this book, I use the phrase "Methodist Church" broadly to refer Methodism, sometimes also referred to as the Methodist Movement. It embraces a wide range of Protestant denominations, including the current United Methodist Church. For more information, see the articles on "Methodism," "List of Methodist Denominations," and "World Methodist Council" available through: *https://www.wikipedia.com*.

Although various histories identify the beginning of the Methodism in Africa with dates later than 1820, the first voyage of African-American Methodist settlers to what would soon become Liberia landed on the 1820 date on Providence Island near today's Monrovia.[2]

This book provides an historical study of the Methodist Movement in Africa, as an encouragement for people to study its important history. The book identifies and celebrates some of the Methodists, including laypeople, pastors, and bishops, who began the spread of the Methodist Movement in Africa.

I hope that the information provided here will motivate further research on Methodism in Africa, as well as on other aspects of international involvement in Africa. This book sees Methodism in Africa as contributing to holistic liberation – that is, economic, political, and spiritual liberation – for all people. It also emphasizes how warmly Methodism is held within the hearts of the many indigenous Africans who follow this powerful form of Christianity.

The book's first chapter celebrates the men and women in Liberia who made up the early Methodist society in Liberia, because with their help the Methodist Church in Africa became a reality.[3] When these men and women started building a new Liberian society, the Methodist Church was part of their society. In other words, for lived experience, there was no separation of church and state. These individuals also played a major role in preparing the way for Methodist missionaries who later came to Africa after 1820.

---

[2] Joseph Saye Guannu. *A Short History of the First Liberian Republic*, 2nd Ed. (Monrovia, Liberia: The Herald Incorporated, 2000).
[3] The fact that the information is about the men, and not the women, even though we know that women were involved equally as the men, the paucity of information on the women makes it impossible to mention them by name. One can only imagine that the women worked along with the men in all the efforts.

Many people are aware of the African-American founders' political role in establishing Liberia, but not many are aware of their theological role as members of Methodist congregations.

The second chapter identifies all those who have served as Methodist bishops in Africa, and who were known as "missionary bishops." The chapter offers a narrative about who those bishops were, with a brief explanation of what each bishop did in building and maintaining the Methodist Church's ministries, including in the rural areas. Those bishops were not the only ones who did that work, but they proclaimed a vision that supported the Church's expansion.

The third chapter introduces the indigenous bishops of Africa. In the 1960s, most of the countries in Africa gained political independence from their European colonizers. The African independence movement that liberated Africa from Europe also brought postcolonial liberation for the Methodist Church. Since 1964, indigenous bishops have been at the helm of leadership for the Methodist Church in Africa. This chapter identifies each of the bishops, beginning with the first person elected.

It was often local leadership that provided the basis for political liberation, including church leadership. For example, in the case of Zimbabwe, Methodist clergy were heavily involved in the independence struggle. The need for local political leadership led to independence, and this need and served as an impetus for the local church leaders.

Chapter four examines the American roots of African Methodism since the 1800s. This chapter looks at the Methodist Church in Africa as originally an American invention, and as an aspect of American religious history that has not been sufficiently explored.

The fifth chapter explores Methodist mission efforts to convert indigenous Africans to Christianity. This chapter looks especially at the Bassa people in Liberia, and it uses them as a microcosm of mission targets of Methodism across Africa. Also, the Bassa people believe that their indigenous African culture prepared the way for Christianity.

An appendix at the end of this book provides a list of all Methodist bishops, both missionary and indigenous, who have served in Africa. This list is important for ensuring that every bishop in Africa is accounted for, and that their efforts are honored.

1

EARLY METHODIST SOCIETY IN AFRICA BEGINNING IN 1820

Methodism is so widespread in sub-Saharan Africa, yet little is known about those who laid the groundwork for this spread of Wesleyan brand of Methodism. The purpose of this book is to highlight some of the people who helped establish the Methodist Church in Africa, beginning in Liberia and Sierra Leone. Another fact of this relationship is the vital role of the United States government and people in establishing the Methodist idea in Africa. Here is one way to learn about the United Methodist Church in Africa. The history is necessary.

Beginning in 1820

It is therefore important to begin the formation of Methodism in Africa as 1820. The story of the Methodist Church in Africa continues, even to this day, and this makes it mandatory for one to keep abreast of the people who started this work. Beginning in the Liberia Annual Conference, the oldest Conference in Africa, there is strong in Africa not only by miracles but hard work by people, with the Holy Spirit as the guide. The beginnings of the Church in Africa will help to also expose the church's role in Africa in the 21st Century and beyond.

Methodism in Africa started with Black people from Britain and the United States of America, who settled in Sierra Leone and Liberia respectively, at various periods in the history of their survival.[1] Both countries are situated on the West Coast of Africa. Both Britain and the United States dealt with post-slavery by sending back to Africa some of those who had been enslaved in these countries.

This was their way of addressing the question of slavery. This way of dealing with slavery from both Britain and the United States of America, led to the formation of the countries of Liberia, between 1820 to 1846, and Sierra Leone in the 18th Century, but gaining political independence in 1960. The Black people from the Western world to Africa settled in these two countries in West Africa.

Sierra Leone started when The Committee for the Relief of the Black Poor in England saw the sufferings of Blacks as being the result of their enslavement, which in turn, made them lack opportunities. Those advocating on the Black people's behalf lobbied to transport the black people back to Africa. Granville Sharp and other abolitionists from England, between 1786-87, were the main advocates for this scheme.[2] Ships from Portsmouth, England left on April 09, 1787, with about 390 people to the West African coast to form a nation in the mountains of lions or Sierra Leone.[3]

Many years later, ships from Norfolk, Virginia took freed Black men, women, and children to the West African coast to form a nation near the mountains of lions, called Liberia, in 1820. The word Liberia has its roots in the notion of freedom or being freed from slavery or enslavement in the United States. Liberia and Sierra Leone were the first two countries where other Blacks who had been enslaved in the West, returned to, to form a country.

---

[1] Sierra Leone, 1787; Liberia, 1820.
[2] Others who helped Granville Sharp in England were: John and Thomas Clarkson, brothers, and Henry Thornton.
[3] The breakdown on of persons on the ship is as follows:

The Blacks who returned to what became Liberia called themselves Americo-Liberians. Their initial efforts, when they arrived in 1820 and beyond, focused on building a Christian-oriented society, like what they had been exposed to in the United States. They wanted to improve their living conditions, to plant churches, and to create institutions that could foster a 'civilized citizenry' in the nation.

This civilization included spreading Christianity to indigenous Africans they would encounter. They had plans to extend their 'civilization' to the indigenous peoples they would meet. The indigenous people were not considered citizens of Liberia during this period. There is no evidence that the indigenous were involved in statecraft. The Americo-Liberians involved themselves also in mission work, spreading the "gospel of Jesus." Spreading the gospel brought pride to the Americo-Liberians, and that pride led to peaceful coexistence with the indigenous Liberians.[4]

The Americo Liberians and their overseas cohorts learned and adopted the laissez-faire approach to governing both in the church and society. The institutions of the church, court, and other public institutions were a static caste system, but Christianity as moral goodness, and a way of preserving their Americo-Liberian culture, took precedence for many of the founding members of the early Methodist Society. Southern Blacks, especially the Roberts brothers, Beverly R. Wilson, and Elijah Johnson, dominated the Liberian political scene, creating southernism in Liberia.[5]

While the American southern Blacks used the agrarian economy, the other Americo-Liberians had northern American ideas, on industry

---

[4] Rev. J. C. Early, Sr. *Personal Memoirs* ... (Atlanta, Georgia, Unpublished Manuscript), 1998.

[5] Joseph Jenkins Roberts, Beverly R. Wilson, and the Roberts brothers, and others, dominated the Liberian political and social scene at its formation in the 1800s (independent, 1847).

and technology.⁶ Their return, they believed, was part of God's plan, crafted in the United States. They were doing everything upon arrival to fulfill this plan of God. They were negotiating with the indigenous population where to call home; they were forming the government; and they were starting churches or denominations they were already familiar with. The settlers hit the ground running, which was their only choice. They could not remain on the vessel that took them. They could no remain homeless. They needed homes and comfortable life. And so, they got to work

Whatever those challenges that constituted God's plan for the return, the shared racial history between Liberia and the United States was a major contributor for the creation of Christianity in Liberia. The United States has its slavery past. And one fact about slavery in the United States that makes it unique, compared to other forms of slavery around the world, is the dehumanizing aspect practiced in the United States on Black people. These were measures used at various points to capture people into slavery. At times, money or goods changed hands. This was business. But the inhumane nature of slavery as practiced in the United States was not what those who may have participated saw. This is not an excuse but another narrative regarding slavery and the role of Africans in the trade.

Christian missionaries – both black and white, from the United States – play a crucial role in the creation of Methodism in Africa. Their mission started in Liberia and extended to other parts of the Continent. Their efforts are worthy of record because, without their role in this process, there would have been less United Methodist influence on the Continent. And because of their sacrifices and hopes, historians must continue to identify and critically evaluate their role in the

---

[6] Sidney Alstrom. *Religious History of the American people* (New Haven, Connecticut: Yale University Press, 1990). See also, James Olson & Heather Olson Beal. *The Ethnic Dimension in American History* (West Sussex, UK: Wiley-Blackman, 2010).

history of the Church. How Methodism came to Liberia and eventually to Africa, is also an aspect of wider Christian history.

Slavery itself, as a man-made institution, creates people of a lesser class, not 'unhuman beings,' and that is nothing new. While the ancient Hebrews worked in Egypt as slaves, they were not considered less than humans. Ancient Egyptian slavery was mostly a working-class form of slavery, rather than slavery based on race, because they were all the same race. Also, the Hebrews were mostly enslaved to build buildings and other forms of infrastructure, and occasionally, as in the case of Joseph and Daniel, they would help in maintaining the status quo, by their own participation or involvement in pharaonic leadership.

This form of slavery was not what took place in the United States, and so the Africans, who returned to Liberia in the 1800s, had totally forgotten everything African, except for their race. They even overlooked the indigenous African peoples who were in Liberia. The Africans who returned to Liberia adopted and maintained their Americanisms in the institutions of leadership.

Those settlers created a marginalized group among poor settlers and indigenous people, despite their creation of a church and a country. As more settlers arrived from the United States and other parts of Africa, the melting pot culture started, and indigenous Liberians experienced the imposed caste system or class system.[7] The Settlers proudly adopted to wear on their sleeves the name Americo-Liberians. In their understanding, the settlers chose this name because they considered America their "ancestral home."

But the name was a contradiction. By maintaining a semblance of Americanism in their outlook, and over the indigenous Liberians and

---

[7] George Klay Kieh, Sr," Causes of the Liberian Coup," 1991,

other Africans, they saw themselves as the 'civilized ones' bringing Christianity to their lost brothers and sisters.

The choice to add "Liberia" meant literally that "these Black Americans in Liberia (Africa) are free." "Liberia" comes from the Latin word for freedom or liberation, namely, *Libertas*. Using the name of American Liberians to refer to themselves meant that indigenous people had to show "respect" to them as their "civilized" brothers and sisters.

By the early 1800s, there had been social divisions even among the African Americans in the USA. This division came about within the north and south by those who assumed that, by taking on the rights and privileges of American citizenship, they were also being connected to 'civilization.'

This book has emerged out of the need to know the history of the Methodist church in Africa from various perspectives. The settlers who founded Liberia were Americans who returned to Africa. The missionaries, who joined them later, came with the hope of seeking (Americo-Liberian) assistance in spreading Christianity to indigenous African peoples. The missionary bishops who served in Liberia and more widely across Africa, have been mentioned in other materials on the Church, but those materials have not been focused on their work in Africa. The current state of the Church in Africa since 1965, when most of Africa became independent from Europe, has also been recognized in other books. But this book provides information on all these pieces of Methodist history in Africa.

More importantly, this book seeks to provide a relationship of this formative ecclesiastical history in Africa, to the United States of America, as a way of drawing some parallel between the religious histories of Africa and the United States. The need to have a history of the Methodist Church in Africa, addressing issues of the episcopacy of the Methodist Church, as well as discussion the formation of the various Methodist Conferences on the Continent, is much needed. This book provides a wide range of information regarding the Methodist Movement in Africa. The book is also a history of the Methodist Church in Liberia.

Again, the Christian history of Liberia started in the 1820s with the coming of freed Africans from the United States. The return of these Africans to this part of Africa could be considered God's plan, despite the numerous challenges and all the negative or positive impacts that plan of God might entail.

Today, we live in a society where we can decide as a people to become one, despite our diverse backgrounds. Despite what any proponent of sectionalism may argue, we live in a world where people come from various backgrounds and experiences. And being together in one geographic location allows for natural cohabitation. But due to individual greed and circumstances, others may propose living in their respective islands. Liberia and the United States share that racial history, both in the formation of the Liberia nation-state and the establishment of Christian religious institutions.

Liberia and the United States of America (hereafter referred to simply as America) have a historical relationship that extends beyond politics. The Methodist Church history in Liberia can bring some clarity to this relationship, which cannot be dismantled. This relationship between both Christian nations clearly underscores the expansion of Christianity with the hope of converting indigenous Africans to Christianity. The use of relationship as an idea does not place the United States over Liberia in any way, but it instead draws on the historical repertoire unique to both countries. This relationship does not undermine Liberia's superiority over America's, but it illumines a discovery of the linked religious history of both peoples.

The Methodist Church has had its presence in Africa since 1830, beginning in Liberia. It has existed as the Liberia Annual Conference since 1834. For that reason, the role of the Methodist Church in Liberia is an important subject for research.

This study specifically emphasizes the role of the bishops elected for the *Liberia Annual Conference*. Bishop Willis Jefferson King, an African-American who was Bishop in Liberia from 1944–1956, gave a general history of the Church in Liberia. His work, *History of the Methodist Episcopal Church in Liberia*, 1957, is one of the major sources of this work. His work deals mainly with the Church in Liberia, with focus on the role the American Church played in developing the Liberia Annual Conference.

Another source is Eugin Koo's *"White" Americans in "Black" Africa: Black and White American Methodist Missionaries in Liberia, 1820-1875*. This work is also a helpful source that shaped my work. Koo's work looks at the missionaries, from the perspective of the race, which was an important factor in their (both White and Black missionaries) selection and commissioning for Liberia. These are two important works of research available on the Church in Liberia.

The book begins with formation of the Methodist Church in Africa from 1822. It takes into consideration the role of missionaries. The Conclusion of the work explores prospects for the Church in Liberia beyond this Century. This history is for posterity to build on.

Some Key Methodist Personalities

Credit goes to the Rev. Daniel Cooker, AME Minister, who served as missionary to the settlers upon arrival at Providence Island, for this growth of Methodist theology in Liberian cultural fabric. Cooker served as chaplain for the settled Africans from America who formed the first Methodist missionary.

> *To Daniel Cooker, a Methodist Minister among the emigrants belong the Imperishable honor of organizing this first Methodist*

Society of the Africans whose home was to be in Africa. Under Cooker's faithful supervision this society maintained an efficient organization for several years.[8]

It was Cooker's missionary efforts that laid the groundwork for the Methodist Church in Liberia –for both AME and Methodist Episcopal Churches. The missionaries who came to Liberia credited Rev. Cooker and the settlers for working hard to build their own Christian society by improving their living conditions, planting churches, and building schools to help them produce an educated population that was also Christian.

This intent of producing good citizens also motivated the settlers and their missionary cohorts to engage the indigenous Liberians such as the Bassa, Kpelle, Kru, and others. Their settlements in places such as Montserrado, Buchanan, Edina, and Harper, to name a few, became steppingstones for building more churches and schools.[9] Among the early Liberians affiliated with the formation of the Methodist Society in Liberia, discussed here are, Stephen Allen Benson, Francis Burns, James Spriggs Payne, John Wright Roberts, Alfred F. Russell, Anthony D. Williams, and Beverly R. Wilson.

Stephen Allen Benson (1816-1865)

Stephen Allen Benson was born in 1816, in Cambridge, Maryland. Little is known about his parents or family connections. He and his family immigrated to Liberia when he was six years old. When they arrived in Liberia, an 'ethnic population' attacked the settlement and Benson, along with his family, was held captive for a few months until an American Colonization Society (ACS) agent secured their

---

[8] Bishop Joseph C. Hartzell, in the *African Mission of the Methodist Episcopal Church*, 27.
[9] Joseph Wold. *God's Impatience in Liberia*. (Grand Rapids, Michigan: William B. Eerdmans Publishing Company, 1968), 54-55.

freedom.[10] Upon his release of Benson and his family, he began his schooling. He obtained all his schooling in Liberia. His affiliation with the Methodist Society prior to 1833 is also not well documented.

However, Benson is remembered largely as a politician and a businessman. His political savviness was recognized when he was first elected to office in 1842, winning a seat on the Colonial Council. He served as a judge until his election as Vice President in 1853, after Liberia gained its independence in 1847. During this time, he was also heavily involved in the Methodist Society in Liberia. President Joseph Jenkins Roberts (a Methodist), and Liberia's first President, declined to seek a fifth term in 1855. This paved the way for Benson to be President. Benson succeeded Roberts.

During his four-term presidency, Liberia saw an expansion of both its internal and external trade with Europeans. During his administration in 1862, the United States recognized Liberia as an independent country. Perhaps his biggest accomplishment was the annexation of the Colony of Maryland, now Maryland County, into the Republic of Liberia in 1857. He also obtained the recognition for Liberia, as an independent country from several other countries.

Benson remained focused on the political culture and its relation to the Christian faith. He advocated for those settlers who wanted to participate in Government to be part of a church, hoping that the principles of Christianity will also prevail in the country, which in turn, will make Liberia a better nation. Benson was fluent in many of the indigenous languages. His leadership both in the church and as President favored a progressive policy toward indigenous Liberians. There is no record that this plan of Benson's was implemented during his lifetime. When he retired from public office returned to

---

[10] The American colonization Society is the organization responsible for sending enslaved Africans back to Africa, in Liberia.

Bassa to live on his farm, in 1863. Stephen Allen Benson died in 1865 in Grand Bassa County.

James Spriggs Payne (1819 -1882)

James Spriggs Payne was both a clergyman and politician. He was born in Richmond, Virginia. His parents moved to the newly formed Liberia colony to settle there when he was nine years old. His father, an ordained Methodist minister, helped in forming the Liberian Methodist society. James attended school in Liberia. In 1840, he returned to the United States to be ordained a Minister in the Methodist church, like his father before him. He returned to Liberia and for several years he was deeply involved in the Methodist church and missionary work. In 1848, he became a Presiding Elder in Liberia. Payne was Superintendent of the Grand Bassa District, a position he held until 1858.[11]

Apart from his religious activities, he was also very interested in politics and economics, and he became a successful writer in both fields. His expertise resulted in the government selecting him as one of the commissioners charged with organizing the details of the separation of the Liberian Commonwealth from the American Colonization Society. He also became the fifth President of Liberia. His life ended in 1882.

Alfred F. Russell (1817-1884)

Alfred Francis Russell was fifteen years old when he and his family left on the brig *Ajax* to Liberia. He was born in Lexington, Kentucky. His parents were Amelie "Milly" Crawford and John Russell. He and his mother were sold to Robert Wickliffe and Mary Owen Todd Russell Wickliffe or Mrs. Polly, as they both affectionately called the mistress. It was an open secret that John Russell (Mary Owen Todd

---

[11] James S. Payne was Liberia's fourth President

Russell's son from her previous marriage with James Russell) engaged in a sexual relationship with Crawford during a summer visit with his grandmother and thereby fathered Alfred.

Alfred's father being white and his mother being a black woman gave him his obvious mixed-race appearance. Alfred F. Russell, who became the fifth President of Liberia, earlier served as missionary to the indigenous people, along with *James H. Stephens.* Both men were officially confirmed or commissioned by the General Conference of 1844 as missionaries to Liberia.

Anthony D. Williams

Anthony D. Williams was distinguished as a preacher and politician in the early Liberian church and society. He was one of the organizers of the Liberia Conference in 1834. He was one of the original settlers who came to Liberia as a missionary. Bishop Elijah Hedding ordained A. D. Williams as both a Deacon and an Elder before reaching Liberia.[12] At the creation of the Conference in 1834, Williams was the only Liberian Elder.[13] Williams presided over the Conference of January 1842 and was elected the first President of the Conference. As founding member of the Conference, he is credited for shaping the structure of the Liberian Conference. The work of Williams is recorded here by Bishop King:

> *The years 1838–1844 … represent the high point in the development of the Mission. The conference seminary was opened in 1839, with Jabez Burton … as its First [President] Principal … At the Conference of 1842, at which the Rev. Anthony D. Williams*

---

[12] Bishop Elijah Hedding (1780–1852) was born in White Plains, New York. Bishop Francis Asbury ordained him Deacon in 1801. In 1805, he became a member of the New England Conference. He is accredited with publishing a *Discourse on the Administration of the Discipline* in 1842. It is not clear how Bishop Hedding and Williams came to know each other.

[13] The other Elders in 1834 were missionaries: Rufus Spaulding and Samuel O. Wright.

presided, the preachers reported 12 charges; 818 full Members, 375 Pupils in the Sunday Schools and 424 pupils in the day schools. An effort was made also to extend the work of the Mission into the hinterland.[14]

The Methodist Church was initially limited to the Liberian settlers and they did not venture beyond the settlers and Americo Liberian settlements to 'win' over the indigenous Liberians. However, this is an impressive feat for Rev. Williams because it was under his administration that the church expanded beyond the *Duu* River and the St. John River, to include indigenous Liberians.

Beverly R. Wilson (d. 1864)

Beverly R. Wilson was born in Norfolk, Virginia. His personal convictions and religious beliefs motivated him to immigrate to Liberia. He was educated, and was well-known, and was included in the "stable families who appeared to enjoy more advantages than were available to most free blacks."[15] Wilson gave up the privileges he had in the Black community of Norfolk, and immigrated to Liberia where he believed he "would be of better service."[16] He served in the Liberian Government, but opted to focus on his ministry full-time. He resigned his positions in government and in the public sector when he realized he could not "attend to the making of laws and the call of God at the same time."[17] Wilson died in 1864.

Although Methodism in Liberia developed with the first group of settlers from the United States, the creation of the Liberia Annual Conference came about only when the first Methodist missionary had died and was replaced by a team of missionaries. Even though

---

[14] Bishop Willis Jefferson King, *History of the Methodist Church Mission in Liberia,* 1955, 23.
[15] Tommy L. Bogger. *Free Blacks in Norfolk: The Darker Side of Freedom,* (University of Virginia Press, 1997), 39.
[16] Bogger, 39.
[17] Ibid.

the Conference started as a mission conference or a launch pad for Methodism in Africa, the Conference continues to contribute to the connectional church through laity and clergy exchange and other forms of networking. The sixteen founding elders of the first conference in 1834 are Solomon Bailey; Richard Boon; David Brown: F. Daveney; Chas Harrison; Remus Harris; Amos Herring; Elijah Johnson; Isaac Legins; Jas. M. Moore; Rufus Spaulding; Daniel Ware, Sr.; Anthony D. Williams; Isaac Welsh; Beverly R. Wilson; and Samuel O. Wright.

The Methodist Church in Liberia began with Liberian settlers and missionaries, both men and women. Given that most of the history about early Methodism in Liberia does not say much about the women who helped their husbands or worked with them, this section will look at the women missionaries, particularly the Black women missionaries. This will be a new introduction to women's role in building the Liberian church and state, even though they do not get much credit as their husbands. Most of the women to be mentioned are from the UMC, the AME, and the AMEZ churches.

Melville Cox (1799-1833) & Methodist Mission Enterprise in Africa 1833-1855

Melvin Cox's arrival in Liberia in 1833 started Methodism in Africa. Recognition of the mission efforts in Liberia started with Melville Cox, who was the first missionary of the Board of the Missions. He was born on November 9, 1799, in Hallowell, Maine. When he was twelve years old, he left school to earn a living. He and his twin brother were "bound out" to earn a living. Cox was self-taught, and he found a job to care for himself and his brother. He loved books.

Prior to his matriculation to Liberia, he was in the Norfolk, Virginia, begging for books for Liberian children. He is reported to have said,

"Missionaries die, books don't."[18] Cox may have realized that the Americo-Liberians, to who he had been specifically sent by the General Church, knew some of them could read, and those who could not read would have the opportunity to read.

Cox was convinced that god called him to mission wok. When he was converted at the age of 34, he wrote in his diary: "God, for Christ's sake forgive my sins and impart to my soul, peace and joy in the Hold Ghost."[19] He became a licensed local preacher first in the New England conference in 1822, the year of his admission to the conference. Due to his ill health, he had to relocate south, to Baltimore, for a relatively warmer climate.

He met Miss Ellen Cromwell in Baltimore, and they were soon married on February 7, 1828. During their marriage, tragedy hit his home, and he lost his wife and daughter. He recorded this experience in his journal as follows: "Surely I have passed a moonless night; the year (1830) has gone. Three brothers-in-law, a dear wife, and sweet child followed each other to the grave in rapid and melancholy succession."[20] The experience did not improve his health, but he remained committed to his calling of becoming a missionary.

By 1833, the Church in the United States had put in place the desire to expand its reach into Africa, and it had been seeking a suitable candidate in this regard. Bishop Paul N. Garber, who was in charge of identifying a suitable missionary candidate for the Church, wrote this: "in 1816 the American colonization Society had been foundation for the purpose of assisting free Negroes to return to Africa, and of founding there a reputable place for them."

---

[18]Brown, Frank, et.al. (Eds). *Norfolk Remembers: Carrying Christ to Africa*, Richmond, Virginia (1932), 10.
[19] Ibid. 11.
[20] Ibid, 10.

Outstanding American leaders sponsored the movement, and it had the endorsement of many religious bodies. It was felt by the churches that the return of the emancipated slaves to Africa would be a missionary enterprise because these Negroes could aid in Christianizing and civilizing the native Africans. Henry Clay had declared "Every emigrant to Africa is a missionary carrying with him credentials in the holy cause of civilization, religion and free institutions."

It is interesting to note that Methodism was taken to Liberia by Negroes emigrants sent there by the American Colonization society. The colony was given the name Liberia – "Land of Freedom" – and the capital was named 'Monrovia' after President James Monroe."[21] In this brief statement from Bishop Garber, it is clear that Cox was committed to his calling, and to the mission in Liberia.

Bishop Garber was also acknowledging the beginning of Methodism in Liberia and the goal of this mission was to "Christianize Africa." It is possible that emancipation of Black people in America was not motivated simply but the negative impact of the act of slavery on those enslaved, but their use as "missionaries" to other parts of the world, especially to Africa, was a key motivation to end slavery.

The General Conference of the Methodist Church in 1820 approved the establishment of t mission in Liberia. Eight years later, the Virginia Conference followed-up on this decision, but there was no one to travel to Liberia. In 1832 at another General conference in Philadelphia, the Bishops approved Cox as missionary to Liberia, with the title of Superintendent.

On November 1, 1832, Cox, at 33, sailed for Liberia on the Jupiter. The trip lasted 126 days. In four days of his arrival, Cox made plans for the new mission. In the plans, there was a call for three new missions. One of the missions was designed to be established in Nigeria.

---

[21] Ibid. 11.

Within each of these missions, the Cox plan included an industrial school, an agricultural school, and a seminary or college. At his first Camp Meeting, 25 persons were converted; and five weeks later, he was able to establish his first worship service in a church. He was a determined missionary and committed to hard work.

However, sickness had its plans. Cox, whose health had always been a big issue, became sick in Liberia. During his sickness, he felt lonely because he did not have many visits from his converts, except an indigenous man who came when Cox was on his 'sickbed.' In his indigenous-influenced English, the man said to him:

"I come to see how you doing. Me be poor man, so me bring you chicken. I not make sheep soup, so you drink it and get well. Me just come to see you. When I go home, I de beg God to make you well."[22] In his diary entry of June 25, Cox wrote, "My body is merely skin and bones." And on the next day, he recorded his last entry, "To God I commit all." On July 21, 1833, his work was complete. [23]

One reason Melville Cox is significant in the history of Liberian Christianity and Methodist history in general, is because he is the first missionary of the Church outside the continent of North America. This is significant because, as Bishop Garber writes, "Today, United Methodists can be proud of this young man who, by his life and death, aroused the conscience of American Methodism to its world task."[24] He is significant for his role in Liberia, because his commitment to his mission was more than his race or health conditions. He was committed to his calling and did not allow limitations to stop him.

---

[22] Norfolk Remembers, 14.

[23] "I have come to see how you are doing. I am a poor man, so I did not bring you chicken. I cannot afford to make you soup that you could consume and get well. I am simply here to see you. When I return to my house, I will pray that God makes you well."

[24] Ibid, 15.

Once in Liberia, he went to work, forming and establishing or organizing the Methodist Church. A year later, the official or formal creation of the Liberia Annual Conference was complete as a Mission Conference. Being a mission conference meant that it was an affiliate conference under the 'tutelage' of the General Church, headquarter in the United States. The General Church had the responsibility or obligation to supply a Presiding Elder and/or Bishop.

2

METHODIST MISSIONARY BISHOPS
IN AFRICA SINCE 1856

This chapter introduces the missionary bishops of Africa, beginning with the first two Bishops of the Liberia Annual Conference. The introduction of each Bishop begins with the date and place of birth, followed by education and year of election as Bishop. The next segment looks at one major contribution of each, and finally, provides the date and place death of said bishop.

Before delving into each Bishop's life in Africa, it is important to discuss the idea of missionary bishop within the Methodist Church. Since 1834, bishops the first two bishops elected were considered missionary bishops, because their jurisdiction, so to speak, was limited to Liberia only, and they had to be consecrated in the United States. The missionary bishops could probably ordain local pastors in the Liberia Conference, and do all the functions of a bishop only in Liberia.

Following the first two bishops whose respective reign lasted from 1834 up to the present, all the bishops who have served in Liberia have not had the same policy for running the church. Their episcopal decisions were different as they were individually different.

But one thing that is similar in all their leadership was the development, maintenance, and continuation of the dependency syndrome, a stigma that was grossly exploited by the last two bishops: Innis and Quire. Each bishop was unique his thinking, personality, and perception. Christian missionaries – both black and white, from the United States – played a crucial role in the creation of Methodism in Africa. Their mission that started in Liberia laid the groundwork for the extension of Methodism through Africa.

The Idea of Missionary Bishops

The idea of Missionary Bishop came as a result of a Decision of the 1856 General Conference, which agreed to allow the "Liberia Mission Conference to elect a bishop to serve there, with the provision that after his election, he should present himself in the USA for Consecration."[1] This idea led to the election of Francis Burns as the first black bishop in the church, followed by John Wright Roberts, as the second black bishop in the Church, even though both had to return to the USA for consecration, according to the General Conference authorization.

Between 1856 to 1965, the Liberian Conference and the conferences in Africa were assigned missionary bishops, elected specifically for Liberia and Africa. Many of these bishops spent most, if not all their years, up to retirement, in the Liberia Annual Conference. Their contributions to the development to the church in Liberia are remarkable, and the obstacles they experienced were also remarkable. Some of the bishops who were placed in charge of the Conference in Liberia area did not go because they were afraid of dying. Imagine leaving the USA for two or three months in Africa, from where you may never return!

---

[1] James Kirby. *Episcopacy in the United Methodist Church* (Nashville, Tennessee: Abingdon Press, 2004), 56.

The missionary Bishops ran the Church. These bishops elected or selected were White and Black men, who had some connection with America. The connection was usually through missionary or emigration. The first two bishops, Francis Burns and John Wright Roberts, were Liberians who had emigrated from the United States of America. Each was elected for the Liberia Conference, but had to be consecrated in the United States by other bishops. Francis Burns came as missionary from New York, and later John Wright Roberts emigrated from Norfolk, Virginia.

Bishop Francis Burns
1809–1863

Francis Burns (elected 1858) was the first Black person to be a bishop in the Methodist Church. He was born in New York on 5 December 1809. He was a product of the public schools in New York. In 1834, he accompanied John Seys as a missionary teacher to Liberia. His membership in the Liberia Conference of the Methodist Episcopal Church was in 1838. He edited the *Africa's Luminary*, the Liberian missionary periodical. He taught at the Seminary in Monrovia and was Presiding Elder or Currently (District Superintendent) for 2 Districts at for 10 years. He presided over the Liberia Conference for 6 years.

He returned to New York and was ordained by Bishop Edmund Short Janes. Bishop Burns was educated, and he put his education into practice in Liberia. Although his episcopacy was limited to the Liberia Conference, no black bishops in the Church had been elected prior to his consecration. Given that the Liberia conference was considered a mission conference, he was considered missionary bishop.

Bishop John Wright Roberts
1812-1875

Bishop John Wright Roberts was elected to succeed Bishop Burns, whose death seemed to have left a leadership vacuum. He followed Burns in promulgating extension of the Conference to interior parts of Liberia, and to develop the conference as a self-supporting mission. However, the Liberia Conference became a Liberia Mission Conference during following his death and with the beginning of Caucasian bishops serving in Liberia.

Bishop Roberts was also the Brother of Liberia's first President, Joseph Jenkins, who was selected based on his work in the church with the Missionaries, particularly Francis Burns. It was Burns who advocated Robert's election, given that Roberts was considered a Liberian. Bishop Roberts died in 1875, with the legacy of being instrumental in creating the Liberia Annual Conference. Although I will list some of their deeds, it will not be possible to present every minute detail of each of the first fourteen bishops of the Liberia Annual Conference.

Anglo-American Missionary Bishops in Africa
1875-1908

The period from 1875–1908 captures the years when Liberia, and the entire Africa, became a place of interest for Mission expansion by the Board of Foreign Missions in New York. Three of those the Caucasian missionary bishops who served in Liberia did so during this period. In this section, I look at the three who lived in Liberia, presided over the Conference, and returned to the United States. The three bishops are: Bishop Gilbert Haven; Bishop William Taylor; and Bishop Joseph Crane Hartzell. This section is important to the history in general because there is much information on their work in Liberia and in Africa. The Methodist episcopacy in Liberia is also rooted in America. This section looks at Americans who became bishops of the church in Liberia. As bishops, they collectively helped to spread the Gospel as they saw fit. The concept of missionary bishop came about at the 1856 General Conference. This Conference decided to authorize the "Liberia Mission Conference to elect a bishop who will serve only in Liberia." The Decision of the General Conference of that year also provided "that after the election, the elected should present himself in the USA for Consecration." Now, Consecration of Bishops is done in Liberia.

Bishop Gilbert Haven
1821-1880

Gilbert Haven came to Liberia as Bishop, succeeding Roberts. He was born on September 19, 1821, in Malden, Massachusetts. As a member of the New England Conference, one of his first assignments was as chaplain during the Civil War. He also served congregations in New York and New Jersey. During the post-civil war reconstruction, he was elected Bishop to serve in Atlanta. His abolitionist views made relations acrimonious with the southern Conference, and he encountered racist attitudes toward peoples of African descent[2]

He was in Liberia in 1875, and his goal was to ensure that the Church reached the native populations of Liberia, and not remain in the cities with the Settlers alone. He designated Rev. C. A. Pitman to visit the interior areas, where he attempted to spread the Church among the native peoples.

Bishop Gilbert Haven succeeded John Wright Roberts as the second Black bishop of Methodism. Bishop Haven was assigned to the Liberian Conference perhaps because of his anti-slavery position in the church. One Newspaper, The Independent, wrote about Haven in 1880, when he died, as follows: "There was not another man in the

---

[2] J. Steven O'Malley, "Haven, Gilbert," in Yrigoyen, Charles & Susan E. Warrick (Eds.). *Historical Dictionary of Methodism*. (Lanham, Md. & London: The Scarecrow Press, Inc., 1996): 105.

American Church who spoke so vigorously, not simply from the freedom of the slave, but for the perfect equality in the State, in the Church, and in the social life of the colored people."[3]

In the 46 days he spent in Liberia, Bishop Haven's anti-slavery disposition allowed him to push for the church to go beyond Monrovia, Buchanan, and Harper, to extend to the interior areas, and to extend membership to the indigenous people. The relatively short duration of his administration or episcopacy was caused by his becoming sick. Some accounts say he was attacked by "malaria."[4]

A lay delegate from South America, he was elected Missionary Bishop for Africa at age 63. He served as Bishop for twelve years. In Africa, his headquarters were in various parts of the Continent, but specifically in Harper, Maryland County, Liberia. He was instrumental in getting many missionaries - both Black and White - to Africa.

The life of Bishop Haven, prior to his going to Liberia as a Missionary Bishop, was centered on abolition. For Haven, slavery was "dishonorable to us as Christians..." [5] By using the word "us" the Bishop could be referring to us, as Christians, one people who proclaim Christ Jesus as Lord and Savior. And by "us" he could be referring to Methodists or Methodist Christians, particularly, the Caucasian "us." The struggle to have a Black bishop who could preside over any of the Conferences in the United States, regardless of nationality or geographic disposition, became of a personal battle for Bishop Haven.

In this effort to get a Black bishop, he suggested to the General Conference of 1867, to give Bishop John Wright Roberts, the Liberia Bishop at the time, to be accorded "full Episcopal powers and

---

[3] *The Independent*, June 8, 1880.
[4] Cox, 1994:12
[5] William Gravely. *Gilbert Haven: Methodist Abolitionist*. (Nashville, Tennessee: Abingdon Press, 1973): 193.

returned to the United States. Although prior to this date, in 1856, the General Conference made provisions for the "election of a missionary bishop for the Liberia Conference," the resolution was either ignored or rebuffed, thereby making Bishop Roberts' Episcopal authority limited to Liberia only.

Bishop Haven was disappointed by this ignorance of the General Conference and he questioned the constitutionality of the office of Missionary Bishop, contending that it was against the basic "Methodist understanding of the general superintendence." He emphasized that restrictions placed on Bishop Roberts "resulted both from a too narrow understanding of the church and from the prejudice against color."[6]

With his advocating that southern Methodist slave owners get rid of their slaves, and the notion of servitude, Bishop Haven would be not only hated in the church, but in the press as well. All of this shows life in these United States at that time. Even following Bishop Roberts' death, Haven came to Liberia to serve as Bishop. Although he did not spend more than a year in Liberia, his legacy in the church in Liberia remains. Through his efforts, the UMC started its vigorous evangelism among the indigenous peoples. His point man was Charles A. Pitman. Bishop Haven died in 1880, with his family at his bedside.

Bishop William Taylor
1821-1902

Bishop Taylor came to Liberia 1855, after his election the year before. He succeeded Roberts. He felt it was an excellent idea for the Liberia Conference to be self-supporting, including the use of its own Discipline. This "aroused a wonderful interest in Africa." Under Bishop Taylor, the ministerial membership of the Conference saw a steady

---

[6] Gravely. *Gilbert Haven: Methodist Abolitionist.* (1973): 194.

rise in number. The first Conference of the Taylor era, in 1893, was held at First UMC, Monrovia. Four Deacons were received at this Conference. James H. Deputie served as Secretary of the Conference.

In 1884, Bishop Taylor became a bishop" to focus on independent ecclesiastical oversight. Although he attended the General Conference in Philadelphia as Bishop, he was born in Illinois on June 1, 1842. His parents were Methodists. He started the Conference Course of Study at 16 and took 11 years to complete. He graduated from Garrett Bible Institute and received the Doctor of Divinity degree in 1875. He entered the Illinois Conference in 1868, transferred to the Louisiana Conference. He was elected in 1896 by the General Church as Missionary Bishop for Africa, with residence in Liberia.

Since the era of Missionary Bishops, there have been six who were of African descent. The Black American missionary bishops can rightly be considered "visiting" bishops, since their place of origin was not Liberia, even though their ancestors were Africans, probably from West Africa. The six Black Missionaries served at various times in Liberia. Their various administrations did not follow in successive patterns, as it will be noted based on their Episcopacy.

According to Kenneth Collins, William Taylor never served in Liberia. Rather, Taylor served in "England, Australia, South Africa, the West Indies, Ceylon, India, and South Africa, with the authority to open missions and to develop Methodist churches anywhere in Africa."[7] But J. Larmark Cox, Sr., in his *Handbook for Conference, District & Local Church Leaders*, 1994, lists Bishop Taylor as one of those who served in Liberia. Cox's records are corroborated by other Methodist scholars. Cox notes:

Rev. William Taylor was elected in 1884 and arrived in Monrovia January 1885 to preside over the Liberia Annual Conference. He made

---

[7] Kenneth J. Collins, in *Historical Dictionary of Methodism*, 206.

his base in Cape Palmas. With his initiative around self-support, Bishop Taylor established Mission Stations on the Cavalla River, the Kru Coast and on the Sinoe, Grand Bassa and St. Paul River Districts. During his episcopacy, almost the entire leadership personnel, lay and ministerial, working under the conference organization was Liberian. He was retired as "Non-effective" by the General Conference and his self-supporting plans were viewed as a complete failure.[8]

Bishop Joseph C. Hartzell
1842-1928

Joseph Crane Hartzell was born on June 1, 1842. He grew up in Moline, Illinois, and attended Illinois Wesleyan College and Garret Biblical Institute.[9] He was admitted to membership in the Central Illinois Conference. He also served churches in New Orleans, where he was also presiding elder. His work with African Americans led to the creation of schools, hospitals. His civic responsibility was to serve on the city's Board of Education. He was elected Bishop at the General Conference in 1896, when the new Congo Mission Conference was born. He organized the Congo Conference, and briefly served in Liberia.

Bishop Joseph Crane Hartzell presided over the 1897 Conference, succeeding Bishop William Taylor. He arrived in Liberia in 1897. He also presided over the Conferences from 1897 to 1902. Bishop Hartzell presided over the Conference again from 1904. Bishop Joseph Hartzell was born on June 1, 1842. He was admitted to membership in the Central Illinois Conference. He also served churches in New Orleans, where he was also presiding elder. His work with African Americans led to the creation of schools, hospitals. His civic responsibility was to serve on the city's Board of Education. He was elected

---

[8] Cox, 13.
[9] Now Garrett Evangelical Theological Seminary

Bishop at the General Conference in 1896, when the new Congo Mission Conference was born. He organized the Congo Conference, and briefly served in Liberia.

For the brief time he was in Liberia, he exhibited exceptional organizational abilities.[10] He was instrumental in recruiting many African Americans interested in Missionary work to join him in Liberia. He and one of the African American missionaries, Ms. Mary Sharp, had a misunderstanding over who had authority over the Conference.[11] This conflict led to the Bishop's transfer from Liberia in 1904.

The 1899 Conference was held from February 8–16, in Harper, Cape Palmas. Bishop Joseph Crane Hartzell, D. D., presided in his capacity as President. The Secretary was Rev. William T. Hagan. The Districts reporting at this Section were: Bassa District, Rev. William T. Hagan, Presiding Elder; Cape Palmas & Cavalla River District, Rev. J. G. Tate, Presiding Elder; Monrovia District, W. T. Hagan; and St. Paul River District, Rev. Isaac N. Holder, PE. Others were Sinoe District, Rev. Joseph W. Bonner, PE, and Madeira Island Mission District, Rev. William G. Smart, PE.

Bishop Hartzell made other strides in Liberia and he was a highly respected Bishop. He retired in the United States and back in the United States, on his 86th birthday.

Bishop Hartzell presided over the 1897 Conference, succeeding Bishop William Taylor. He also presided over the Conferences from 1897 to 1902. Bishop Hartzell presided over the Conference again from 1904. He was admitted to membership in the Central Illinois

---

[10] Cox, J. Larmark. *Handbook for Conference, District, & Local Church Leaders*. (Lithonia, Georgia: SCP/Third World Literature Publishers, 1994): 13

[11] Bishop Hartzell recruited Mary Sharp; an African American Woman to work specifically with the Kru people in New Kru Town, a suburb of Monrovia. Ms. Sharp was interested in providing independent leadership to the Kru people, so that they would be able to work in the church and understand its teachings or doctrines. The funding however was lacking, and that set Ms. Sharp on "fire." The Bishop was later transferred to the United States.

Conference. He also served churches in New Orleans, where he was also presiding elder. His work with African Americans led to the creation of schools, hospitals. His civic responsibility was to serve on the city's Board of Education. He was elected Bishop at the General Conference in 1896, when the new Congo Mission Conference was born. He organized the Congo Conference, and briefly served in Liberia. On his 86th birthday, thieves assaulted and robbed him near his home, in Blue Ash, Ohio, and died because of his injuries.[12]

Bishops Haven, Taylor, and Hartzell were three prominent Methodist Bishops. It is important that each person chose their assignment. Not that they had to abandon their assignments, but their outlook on life was beautiful. For example, Bishop Haven was an abolitionist. He was one of those bishops who felt like John Wesley felt, when he served as a Missionary to the indigenous Americans and black people who were enslaved. In these people, Wesley was delighted that the enslaved and uncivilized were more than their masters. Haven interest in abolition help propelled him into the episcopacy accomplishments in the church is remarkable and incredible. Gilbert Haven (1872), William Taylor (1884), and Joseph Crane Hartzell (1896) will be discussed more fully.

These bishops and those who came after them later may have spread the Wesleyan Theology in Africa. These Caucasian Bishops sought local episcopacy supervision as a grave concern.[13] Their respective life story speaks to the expansion of the Methodist ideal that expands ethnicity, cultures, and nationalities. Moreover, their service in Africa speaks to the fact that the Gospel of Christ is not limited to Europeans only, but also to Africans as well.

---

[12] Barbara E. Campbell. "Hartzell, Joseph Crane," in Yrigoyen, Charles & Susan E. Warrick (Eds.). *Historical Dictionary of Methodism.* (Lanham, Md. & London: The Scarecrow Press, Inc., 1996): 104-5.
[13] The two Bishops: Francis Burns and John Wright Roberts served from 1855-75.

African-American Bishops
1904-1965

When the "era" of the Caucasian missionaries ended, the general church decided to recruit Black Africans in America or African Americans, both male and female, to serve in Liberia. The church wanted people who could travel outside of the settlements into the rural areas, where local settlers had often refused to go.

Even though the first two bishops of the Conference, Francis Burns and John Wright Roberts were African Americans, it had been established that they were Liberian citizens, losing their American citizenship. Even so, those Black Missionary Bishops were African American men. Bishop Burns and Bishop Roberts were both Liberian citizens who held the post. The bishops were elected in the United States and assigned to Liberia.

This chapter focuses on those African American Bishops who did not take a Liberian citizenship but were elected, consecrated, and assigned to the Liberian conference.

Bishop Isaiah Benjamin Scott
1854-1931

Bishop Scott was born in Midway, Kentucky, on September 30, 1854. His parents were Benjamin and Polly Anderson Scott. His father, Benjamin, was born free and was identified with the "underground railroad" before the Civil War. He went to private schools in Frankfort, Kentucky. He later attended Clark College (Clark Atlanta University), and Central Tennessee College, Nashville.

He was married to Mattie J. Evans in May 1881, and this union was blessed with six children. His ministry started on trial in the Tennessee Conference of the Methodist Episcopal Church in 1880. He was later transferred to the Texas Conference in 1881, and ordained elder in 1884. His appointments include Nashville Circuit in 1880; Trinity, Houston, 1881-2; St. Paul, Galveston, 1883. In 1893, New Orleans University conferred on him the DD degree.

He was elected in 1904 as missionary Bishop and assigned to Liberia. His residence was in Monrovia. He retired in 1916 and moved to Nashville. Bishop Scott is special to Liberia. His episcopacy ended the era of Caucasian missionary bishops. His focus was expanding the church to areas where his predecessors could not reach. His wealth of knowledge on the Methodist Church in general made him an asset bishop because he was able to provide training in Methodism for the clergy and other members of the Conference. He died on 4 July 1931. His burial place is in Nashville.

Bishop Matthew Wesley Clair
1865- 1943

Matthew Wesley Clair was born in Union, West Virginia on 21 October 1865. His father was Anthony Clair, and his mother was Ollie Green Clair. He was converted at the age of 15 in Charleston. During this time, he served a dishwasher at Hale House. The Hale House was belonged to Dr. John P. Hale, the Mayor responsible for making Charleston into West Virginia's Capital in 1871.

Bishop Clair attended and graduated from Morgan College, Baltimore, in 1889, and received DD and LLD Degreed from there. He also received honorary degrees from Howard and Wilberforce Universities. His first wife was Fannie Walker, who predeceased him. This union was blessed with five sons. He later remarried on November 2, 1925 Eva F. Wilson.

His ministerial career started with the Washington Conference on trial in 1889 and was ordained Elder in 1893. He served in the following appointments: Harper's Ferry, West Virginia, from 1889-1893; Staunton, Virginia, from 1893-1896; Ebenezer Church, from 1896-

1897. He later served as Presiding Elder for the Washington District, from 1897-1902; Ashbury Church, Washington, from 1902-1919. He also served as District Superintendent of the Washington District, 1919-1920. He was elected Bishop in 1920 and assigned to Liberia. Traveling by hammock with African carriers, he traversed jungle and veld and preached to the natives through Glebe and Mano dialect [language] interpreters."[14]

While in Liberia also, the President of Liberia appointed him to the board of Education. He also served as the one of the members of the American Advisory Commission of the Booker Washington Agricultural and Industrial Institution or Liberia. He returned to the United States after eight years in Liberia as Bishop. He later served as Bishop of the Covington, Kentucky area bishop for two quadrennials, before retiring.

Bishop Alexander Priestly Camphor
1865–1919

Alexander Priestly Camphor lived from 1865 – 1919. During these 54 years, he was an educator, missionary, bishop, and a husband. He was born on August 9, 1865 in Soniat, Jefferson Parish, Louisiana, USA. Little is accounted for about his parents in this writing because of the paucity of information on his early life. When he was a child, his mother also had other children, so she "gave" him in care of Rev. Stephen Priestly, her pastor, to educate him. Pastor Priestly needed him badly because he wanted a boy to live in his house, and Alexander was on time. Alexander Camphor adopted the name Priestly as his middle name, in honor of Rev. Priestly.

Alexander got a solid education. He attended Leland University for a year (1879-1880), New Orleans University for two years (1880-1882). He later attended and graduated from Gammon Theological

---

[14] Nolan B. Harmon. *Encyclopedia of Methodism*, 511.

Seminary between 1893 and 95; he did additional studies at Union Theological Seminary and Columbia University in New York. In the summer of 1912-1914, he was a student at the University of Chicago. His education did make way for him. He became Professor of Mathematics at New Orleans University.

His ministerial pursuits started in the Delaware Conference of the Methodist Episcopal Church, with his pastoral leadership staring at Germantown, Pa. He later moved to Orange, New Jersey as Pastor there in 1896. During his pastoral experience, he felt inadequate and incomplete in ministry because he felt called to mission's work. In 1897, he and his wife moved to Liberia as missionaries. He served as founding President of the College of West Africa, a glorified high school, until 1907. While he was in Liberia, he served as Vice Consul for the American Embassy near Monrovia. He returned to the USA in 1908 and became President of the Central Alabama Institute in Birmingham. He remained in this post until 1916, when he was elected Bishop and assigned to Liberia. His title was "Bishop for Africa."

In Liberia, as missionaries, Camphor and his wife, Mamie Weather Camphor, were commissioned by the board of missions in 1896. At the College of West Africa, they were able to build a large enrollment, with 30 indigenous Liberians.[15] They were focused on educating Liberian children, whether they belonged to the settlers or to the indigenous people children. Bishop Camphor died on December 11, 1919.

Bishop Willis Jefferson King
1886–1976

Willis Jefferson King was born in Rose Hill, Texas on 1 October 1883. His parents were: Anderson W. and Emma Blackshear King. No

---

[15] Alexander Priestley Camphor, *Missionary Story Sketches folklore from Africa*, The Black Heritage Library collection (Freeport, New York: Books for Libraries Press, First published 1909, Reprinted 1971), 9.

information about his parents is available. His post elementary and high school educational journey took him to Wiley College, Texas, from where he obtained the bachelor's degree. His graduate and PhD degrees were obtained from Boston University. He was awarded DD from Wiley College in 1933 and from the University of Liberia in 1950.

His first wife was Parmella J. Kelly in 1913. She predeceased him on1943. This union was blessed with three girls. He remarried in 1944 to Emma Arnold., and they remained married until his death. His ministry started in the Texas conference in 1908. He became an elder in 1913. His pastoral assignments included: Greenville, Texas, 1908-10; 4th Church, Boston, 1912-1915; St. Paul Church, Galveston, Texas, 1915-1917; and Trinity Church, Houston, Texas 1918. In addition to this, he also taught Hebrew Bible at Gammon Theological Seminary 1918-1930. He later served as President between 1932-1944. He was elected Bishop in 1944 and served in Liberia from 1944-1956. He also served the New Orleans as Bishop from 1956-1960.

He is famous as an author for the following publications: *The Negro in American Life*, 1926; *History of Methodist Mission in Liberia,* 1951; *Personalism in Theology*, 1943; and *Christian Bases of World Order*, 1943. He also contributed to the *History of American Methodism*, 1964. Bishop King retired and lived in New Orleans. Bishop King died on June 17, 1976. A few days later, on June 29, his wife, Mrs. Emma Arnold Kind, died.

In Liberia, Bishop King was instrumental in training local Liberian youths for the church. He recruited gifted missionaries from within the African American community, and serious Caucasian missionaries. He and President William VS Tubman, a Methodist, got along very well. He was the president's Bishop, and so, whatever Bishop King wanted, it was done. Prior to his retirement from Liberia, he was awarded the Humane Order for African Redemption, with the rank of Grand Knight, Liberia's highest honor bestowed on a person. Bishop Prince A. Taylor succeeded him.

Bishop Prince Albert Taylor, Jr.
1907-1996

Prince A. Taylor, Jr. was born in Hennessey, Oklahoma, on 27 January 1907. His parents were Prince Albert, Sr., and Bertha Ann (Littles) Taylor. His educational journey started in Hennessey, and continued to Austin, Texas, where he enrolled at Sam Houston College, obtaining his bachelor's degree in 1931. He was also a graduate of Gammon Theological Seminary, Atlanta; Union Theological Seminary/Columbia University, New York in 1940. He earned a doctorate in Education (Ed.D.) from New York University in 1948. Honorary doctorate degrees were obtained from Rust College, Mississippi; Gammon Seminary, Atlanta; and Dickinson College. Others include Philander Smith College and the University of Puget Sound.

He and Annie Belle Thaxton were married in July 1929. This union was blessed with one daughter. Bishop Taylor's ministerial career started in 1931 when he was ordained elder in the North Caroline Conference. He served as pastor in Kernersville; Northwest Greensboro Charge; St. Thomas, Thomasville; East Calvary, New York City. He was interim Pastor at St. Mark Church in New York.

He was elected Bishop on June 16, 1956, and promptly assigned to Liberia. He spent eight years in Liberia before returning to the USA and assigned to the New Jersey Area. His years in Liberia solidified Methodism and revel in Liberian politics as deeply as possible. He was instrumental in putting in place the independence framework for Liberia's indigenous clergy to fill the episcopacy. Bishop Taylor felt it was useless for the General Church to send Americans – whether of African or Caucasian descent from the United States – to serve as Bishop in Liberia. He had helped to prepare several competent and qualified men and women from the country. He saw need for clergy in Liberia to run the church. In Liberia, the logic for the local Liberians to elect their own episcopal head from among the available clergy. Bishop Prince Taylor, the last of the Bishops in this missionary category.

3

METHODIST CHURCH IN AFRICA:
OVERVIEW SINCE 1800

On the continent of Africa, the mission of the Methodist Church and its predecessor bodies has developed through missionaries, mostly from the U.S. but also from Europe. Except for Liberia as a colony for freed slaves, there was no mutual benefit from migration towards and from the U.S. as in Europe or partly in Asia.

The mission of the church in Africa was not limited to the preaching of the Gospel. Two other main elements were part of a holistic approach: educational endeavors in building up of schools, from elementary schools up to professional and university education; and health care with clinics and dispensaries. Churches, and among them the Methodists, helped to raise a generation of indigenous leaders in church and state. The Church in Africa has remained dependent on outside support in both personnel and finances. This is sad because currently, African Methodism should have developed beyond dependent on foreign support.

What follows will be limited to sub-Saharan Africa. The mission in North Africa always belonged to the European region. Except for Liberia (Methodist Episcopal Church, 1822/1832) and Sierra Leone (United Brethren, 1855), the Methodist mission from the U.S. in sub-Saharan Africa began towards the end of the 19th and the early 20th century.

In 1920, General Conference wanted to do away with missionary bishops whose jurisdiction was limited to their electoral region outside the U.S., but a similar limitation was re-introduced in 1928 when General conference gave authority to central conferences to elect their respective bishops. In 1920, the Methodist Episcopal Church established a central conference for South Africa, which comprised its conferences in the Southern part of Africa: Angola, Congo (today DRC, Southern region), Mozambique, and Southern Rhodesia (today Zimbabwe). Liberia was not part of that central conference. The central conference first met in Old Umtali, Rhodesia, and the bishop resided in Cape Town.

After the merger of 1939, a provisional central conference met in 1943, which included all annual conferences in sub-Saharan Africa (Liberia was only present in 1943). In 1948, it became the Africa Central Conference. In 1956, it was subdivided into two episcopal areas. In 1960, a third bishop was authorized, but not elected. In 1964, the central conference subdivided into four episcopal areas: Angola, Congo, Mozambique, and Rhodesia (Zimbabwe). Liberia was authorized to organize into a central conference of its own and elect its bishop.

Up until the Methodist union in 1968, the Evangelical United Brethren Church supported ministry in Sierra Leone and Nigeria. In Sierra Leone, the EUB mission became autonomous in 1968. In Nigeria, it began as cooperation with the Sudan United Mission, forming the Muri Church in 1965. In 1980, these autonomous churches in Sierra Leone and Nigeria joined the Methodist Church. General Conference then authorized the creation of a West Africa Central Conference, comprising Liberia, Sierra Leone, and Nigeria.

In 1968, a single central conference was created for sub-Saharan Africa, called Africa central conference, with all the conferences from the former Methodist Church: Angola, Liberia, Mozambique, Rhodesia (Zimbabwe), and Zaire (DR Congo). It met in Botswana in 1968.

In 1984, the Evangelical Episcopal Church of Burundi joined The United Methodist Church and became part of the Africa central conference.

In 1992, General Conference authorized the creation of a Zaire (today Congo) central conference. The Africa central conference kept its original name, now comprising Angola, Burundi (today East Africa), Mozambique, and Zimbabwe. Thus since 1992, there are three central conferences in sub-Saharan Africa: (1) Africa; (2) West Africa; (3) Congo.

Africa Central Conference

The Central Conference of Africa kept its name from the time when there was one single central conference for all sub-Saharan Africa, the Liberia Mission Conference. The growth of the Church in Africa has led to five Episcopal Areas for Southern Africa alone. In Angola, there are two Episcopal Areas; in Mozambique; in Zimbabwe; and in Kenya. Tanzania recently joined the Conferences in this part of Africa. Through his efforts, the current missionary to Tanzania, David Rhodes, has connected the Alabama-West Florida Conference with the Tanzanian Conference. Even though there is currently on Episcopal Leadership in Tanzania, it belongs to one of the Conferences in East African.

In 1920 at the creation of the first central conference for the southern part of Africa, the South Africa Central Conference, the bishop was a general superintendent", a U.S. citizen, residing in Cape Town, South Africa. The mission also extended to the Transvaal (Union of South Africa). In 1936, the central conference used its right to elect its own bishop, the U.S. missionary Springer.

After the subdivision of the central conference into four episcopal areas in 1964, each of the countries Angola, Mozambique, and Rhodesia (Zimbabwe) were supervised by its own bishop for the first time, as was the Congo which became a central conference on its own in 1992. In Angola, a missionary from Norway was elected as bishop. Bishop Dodge (U.S.) continued in Rhodesia. In Mozambique an indigenous pastor, Zunguze, was elected as bishop.

With the creation of the United Methodist Church (UMC) in 1968, all bishops became general superintendents of the church. The first session of the Central Conference of Africa was held in Botswana, 1968. The newly elected bishop for Rhodesia (Zimbabwe) was also an indigenous pastor, Muzorewa.

In 1984, the Evangelical Episcopal Church of Burundi joined the UMC and became part of the central conference of Africa. Its bishop became a United Methodist bishop. Due to the political situation, he fled to Kenya in 1994. Thus, the mission of the UMC began to spread to Kenya, Rwanda, Tanzania, Uganda, and Southern Sudan. These countries, except Tanzania, became part of the East Africa Annual Conference and episcopal area.

Due to the political situation in Angola, General Conference 1988 authorized an additional bishop for the central conference of Africa. It allowed the creation of a second episcopal area for Angola. Thus, the central conference of Africa has five episcopal regions: West Angola, East Angola, East Africa, Mozambique, and Zimbabwe.

The mission of the United Methodist Church and its predecessor Methodist bodies began in the following years: Angola (1885), Botswana (2001), Burundi (1984 joining the UMC), Kenya (1990), Malawi (1987), Mozambique (1892), Ruanda (1996), South Africa (1919 Transvaal), South Sudan (2005), Uganda (1990), Zambia (1984), Zimbabwe (1897).

Congo Central Conference

The central conference of Congo was established in 1992. Before that date, the Democratic Republic of Congo (formerly called Zaire) belonged to the central conference of Africa (after 1939), respectively the central conference for South Africa (1920-39).

The Methodist mission in the DR Congo has several origins. In the Methodist Episcopal Church, Bishop Taylor started his plan for a self-supporting mission from Angola and reached the Belgian Congo in 1886. But the mission endeavors came to an end in 1896. The U.S. missionary Springer traveled through Zambia and the Belgian Congo towards Angola on his way to the U.S. As he returned to Africa, he opened a mission in the southern part of the Belgian Congo, establishing a first mission station in Lukoshi in 1911. In 1915, it became the Congo Mission Conference. In 1936, the central conference of South Africa elected Springer as its bishop.

The Methodist Episcopal Church South entered the Belgian Congo along the Congo-river and established its first mission station in Wembo Nyama in the central part of the country. At the union of 1939, both mission fields became part of the Methodist Church and of the central conference of Africa under the leadership of Bishop Springer up to his retirement in 1944. Other U.S. bishops continued oversight for the next twenty years.

In 1964, the central conference of Africa was authorized to elect four bishops, one of them for the Congo. With John Wesley Shungu, it elected for the first time a Congolese pastor. General Conference 1980 authorized the election of an additional bishop. The southern part (Shaba, later Katanga province) became a separate episcopal area. In 1988, General Conference authorized again the election of an additional bishop. The Shaba (later Katanga province) was subdivided into two episcopal areas, South Congo, and North Katanga.

All the other ten provinces of the country remained one episcopal area despite the extension of the mission to many new regions, including the capital Kinshasa. In 2012, General Conference authorized a fourth episcopal area for the central conference of Congo. Thus, the two episcopal areas of Central Congo and East Congo were created.

Each episcopal area of the DR Congo has also extended into neighboring countries: Central Congo into the Republic of Congo (Brazzaville) and Gabon; East Congo into the Central African Republic; North Katanga into Tanzania; and South Congo into Zambia.

West Africa Central Conference

The central conference of West Africa was established in 1980. Before that date, the United Methodist presence in West Africa was reduced to Liberia.

The Methodist mission in Liberia is by far the oldest of all missions outside the U.S. As we have seen, it began in 1822 through initiatives of individuals among former slaves, under the auspices of the "American Colonization Society." Again, the name of the colony was *Liberia* in honor of the new-found freedom. In 1833, it received support by the sending of a first missionary who unfortunately died within five months of his arrival. In 1856, General Conference made provisions for the election of missionary bishops, limited in their jurisdiction to their electing region. A missionary was elected in 1858. His successor as missionary bishop in 1863 was a former slave who had arrived in Liberia in 1829, John W. Roberts. After his death in 1875, the succeeding bishops again came as visiting bishops from the U.S. In 1904, General Conference elected an African American as "missionary bishop" who again took residence in Liberia.

Between 1898 and 1939, the Portuguese Island of Madeira became another place of presence for the Methodist Episcopal Church, at some time even as residence of the bishop having supervision for Africa. The 1940 General Conference of the Methodist Church authorized to establish a provisional central conference for Africa which included Liberia. But delegates from Liberia were only present at the first meeting in 1943. In 1964 General Conference authorized Liberia to become either an autonomous church or to form a central conference with the right to elect a bishop. The annual conference of Liberia in 1965 opted for the latter.

In 1980, the autonomous church in Sierra Leone (former United Brethren mission since 1853; discussing a union with British Methodists and Anglicans in the 1960s) and the Muri Church in Nigeria (a united church with former United Brethren mission since 1922) joined the United Methodist Church. General Conference therefore authorized the creation of a West Africa Central Conference, comprising Liberia, Sierra Leone, and Nigeria. At first, it had two episcopal areas. In 1992, General Conference authorized an additional episcopal area and a first bishop for Nigeria was elected.

In 2004, the autonomous Methodist Protestant Church of the Ivory Coast (former British Methodist mission since 1914) joined the United Methodist Church. From 2008 onwards, the central conference of West Africa was officially comprised of four episcopal areas. The mission of the United Methodist Church and of predecessor Methodist bodies began in the countries belonging to the central conference in the following years: Cameroon (2000), Ivory Coast (1914), Liberia (1822), Nigeria (1922), Senegal (1995), and Sierra Leone (1853).[1]

Brief History of Methodism in Sierra Leone

The Methodist Church in Sierra Leone started as United Brethren in Christ in 1855. It merged with the Evangelicals in 1946 and became the Evangelical United Brethren Church. In 1968 it merged with the Methodist Church becoming the United Methodist Church. During this time, all presiding bishops were from the USA.

---

[1] *http://www.umc.org/who-we-are/history-of-the-united-methodist-church-in-africa/, accessed on 12/18/2018.*

In 1973 the church assumed autonomy with the first indigenous bishop, Dr, Ben A. Carew. Carew, for his part, made tremendous efforts to allow the connection work. However, his death that year left many of his dreams unfulfilled.

In 1979, Rev. Thomas S. Bangura, was elected to succeed Dr. Carew. The growth of the church in Sierra Leone is one we can attribute to the efforts of Carew and others. The current strength of the Conference is 100 thousand, with nearly 7000 probationary members, and 13000 members. The United Methodist Church in Sierra Leone operates 213 primary (elementary) and 20 secondary or high schools. It runs 11 maternity and health center throughout the country. There is an eye hospital, fully staffed.

Bishop Joseph C. Humper is the third indigenous Sierra Leonean to become Bishop of the Sierra Leone Conference. He was elected to the episcopacy on August 14, 1992, by the West Africa Central Conference. He was born Joseph Christian Humper, in Bonthe Sherbro (the village of Somway-Kenema), Gone Section, Sitia Chiefdom, Southern Province of Sierra Leone, West Africa. Little is given about his childhood and early upbringing.

His higher education included the Bible Training Institute in Bo at Bo Teacher's College. His training in theology was completed at Trinity College, Legon, Ghana (where he received a Certificate in Theology-First Class), the University of Ghana at Accra (Diploma in Theology-First Class); Fourah Bay College, University of Sierra Leone (B.A.); and Union Theological Seminary in New York City. .

He worked as teacher and pastor in a variety of settings, and other related positions in the Sierra Leone area, including Conference Youth Director, Director of the Ministerial Training Program, Bishop's Chaplain, Conference Council Director, and Associate Executive Secretary of the West Africa Central Conference. Volunteer positions in the Conference include Registrar of the Board of Ordained

Ministry, Annual Conference Secretary. He was ordained deacon and elder by Bishop Benjamin A. Carew.

He also served on a few committees and organizations related to the church. He held such positions as President, Council of Churches in Sierra Leone (CCSL); President, Inter-Religious Council of Sierra Leone (IRCSL); and Honorary President, World Conference on Religion and Peace. He was Conference Council Director when elected and assigned to the Sierra Leone Area. He served there until his retirement in 2008. Joseph C. Humper is married to Nancy Mamie Humper; they have four children: James, Josephine, Joseph, and Marvel. The current Bishop is John Yambasu.

At the 1980, the Liberia Annual Conference experienced a major political setback. The Bishop, Bennie D. Warner, was deposed from his position as Vice President. He was attending a Council of Bishops Meeting when the Liberian Government of President William R. Tolbert, Jr., a Baptist Prelate, was overthrown. Bishop Warner, as Vice President of Liberia, automatically became an enemy of the military Government. The Government threatened him that he would be arrested and persecuted if he returned to Monrovia. Since he could not return to Liberia, fearing for his life, a new Bishop had to be elected. Some members of the Conference wanted the Bishop to remain in his position as Bishop in Exile, but others felt it better to have the resident bishop reside in the country. At a Central Conference held in Monrovia, the Church elected Arthur F. Kulah.

The West Africa Central Conference (WACC) in 1992 discussed a draft *Book of Disciple* that would reflect the experiences of the Conferences involved. The Book of discipline is the United Methodist Church's law book. It is the main book, in addition to the Bible, that the church uses to govern itself throughout the world. But the Book was a creation of Methodists who were educated in Western tradition, and were not necessarily familiar with the traditions, customs, and cultures of non-Western peoples.

As a result, the Draft of the "WACC Book of Discipline was accepted by the Conference for onward transmission to the various Annual Conferences for study and endorsement in principle."[2] This document is necessary because, in it, one can be certain that the authors have considered their respective contexts as African peoples, and as nation states with different constitutional perspectives. This document has been pending approval from the General Conference.

The church continues to grow in all aspects of its ministries. It has become a pattern, and in Africa, United Methodism is still going strong, like "Johnny Walker" whisky. Evangelism and Mission efforts continue unabated in countries such as Tanzania. Ideas for United Methodism in Tanzania, a predominantly Islamic Republic in southern Africa, started with efforts by Methodist Christians from Congo. As the growth of the church in Tanzania has taken deep roots with Eric and Liz Sword, along with David Rhodes, the Alabama West Florida Conference has teamed up with Tanzania for the development of the Church in that sovereign African nation.

The information provided in this book about Tanzania comes from the Website of the Alabama West Florida Conference. The Alabama West Florida Conference and the Tanzania Annual Conference formed a partnership which became formal on June 4, 2019, at Frazer UMC, Montgomery, Alabama. The partnership gave birth to the concept of "Teaming with Tanzania" (TWT). TWT is the common agreement between the Alabama West Florida Conference and the Tanzanian Conference for cooperation and partnership.

---

[2] Smith-Eastman, Rev. Marie. "Report of the Delegation to the West Africa Central Conference Held with the Sierra Leone Annual Conference UMC, Moyomba, August 11-16, 1992," *Conference Journal of the 160th Session of the Liberia Annual Conference, UMC*, Monrovia, Liberia (July 5-11, 1993), 214.

"Teaming With Tanzania"

"In March of 2018, a team of 10 people from the Alabama-West Florida Conference traveled to Tanzania to explore possibilities for greater support of the United Methodist Church in Tanzania. From this trip **Teaming with Tanzania** *was established to develop a long-term partnership between the Alabama-West Florida Conference and the United Methodist Church of Tanzania. This partnership of discipleship and shared ministry supports ministries that are self-sustaining and focused on leadership development, economic development, and capacity development."*[3]

"Through this multi-tiered, multi-year Teaming with Tanzania mission campaign, individuals, small groups, local churches, and districts within the Alabama-West Florida Annual Conference are encouraged to get involved and partner with the people of Tanzania. In addition to a relational ministry partnership, three areas of support are available."[4] *(For more details, see the prior-noted link.)*

Worship and Evangelism through the Building of Churches

"As the Gospel continues to spread in Tanzania and new United Methodist churches are established, church buildings are needed to support these congregations. By supporting the construction of a church building, people are helping provide a place for the people of Tanzania to worship, and they are promoting evangelism around the world. The cost of church building projects range from $25,000 for a smaller village church to $50,000 for a larger town church.

---

[3] Susan Hunt. "Teaming with Tanzania" *https://www.awfumc.org/tanzania*, accessed 8/15/2019:6:19 p.m.
[4] Ibid.

This cost includes the land purchase, church construction, and a parsonage. (Again, for more information, see the prior noted link."[5]

Education and Development through Wesley College

"Located in the Mwanza Region of northern Tanzania, Wesley College is a United Methodist related institution that offers programs in theology and adult education. By sponsoring student scholarships, providing technology and resource needs, and helping with capital for future development, donors support the training and education of current and future leaders in Tanzania, and they promote ministry that is long-term and self-sustaining."[6]

Training & Development Opportunities

"Opportunities are available for qualified individuals to provide short-term training sessions in Tanzania. Teams of five to eight people provide training in specific areas such as: entrepreneurial and small business training, economic empowerment, pastoral training, laity training, discipleship training, children's ministry leadership training, Christian education training, and vocational training."[7]

This is another example of the Methodist Church's involvement in Africa. It which will provide academic support to people in that area, as well as assist in other areas such as health, worship, and business ideas.

---

[5] Ibid,
[6] Ibid,
[7] Ibid.

4

AFRICAN METHODISM & AMERICAN ROOTS SINCE 1800

To examine the background of American Religious history, it will be appropriate to examine the African and European backgrounds that form American religion. In so doing, one may give specific attention to the environments in which they flourished. To discuss Liberian Christian history in context of American religious history is to also take into consideration the symbiotic development. As such, specific consideration is given to the Reconstruction Era, the African American Preacher, and the reversal of reconstruction.

Furthermore, Protestant polarities, non-Protestant immigrants, the Civil Rights Movement, and modern Protestant conservatism are all basic themes of modern American religious history which have lasting impact on African theological discourse. Thus, the chapter will also consider the origins of various denominations, with little focus on their structure and teachings.

African Christianity relates to the Christian history of the United States in that it started with both Black and White missionaries, Immigrants, and non-Immigrants, who saw the desire to save the Africans from hell. By studying the ideologies and personalities that formed African Christianity, specifically the Methodist Church, one will see the parallel of a transformed religious context, which paved the way for coexistence and dialogue. To recognize the continuous opportunities that exist for religious dialogue among Christians and non-Christians in the United States is also a similar need for Africa. This is necessary because both historiographies highlight the movers and shakers of the respective religious culture. Exposure to American religious historiography helps to dissect the indigenous and settler cultures in Africa.

The Methodist Church in Africa is where it is today because of the role played by the Methodist churches in America. The history of the Church in Africa is filled with Americans – both Black and White – who laid the groundwork. The African church is alive today because of the American involvement. This chapter identifies this connection and discusses it. The indigenous peoples of Africa were the main mission targets of the Missionary movement of Europe and the United States in the 19th century. The Methodist missionaries to Africa were mainly people from the United States.

The Americans have been focused on expanding the Wesleyan ideology or the Wesleyan quadrilateral. The Wesleyan quadrilateral, it can be argued, is applicable and appropriate for the countries in Africa where the United Methodist Church currently exists. It may be the application of the Wesleyan ideologies that have kept these countries surviving.

The Wesleyan quadrilateral focuses on experience, tradition, reason, and Scripture as the basis for human interaction and connection to the divine. In broader African ways of life, experience brings to bear the day-to-day realities of existence. Whether "good" or "bad", or whether "hard" or "easy," existence in such contexts is based on experience. One can cope or not cope with the daily challenges of life, and therefore, this aspect of Wesleyanism is account with the African way of life.

The tradition of the Church is also captured in the experience and the tradition of African peoples. The church itself is an institution with formal rituals and sacrifices that speak to developing one fully into human, and to be fit for God's kingdom. Whether it is considered a kingdom of God, consciously or subconsciously, the traditions of the church serve as substitutes of the indigenous rituals and sacrifices of the people.

In the Western word, those African practices are revered in religions such as Candomble, Santeria, Sevi Lwa (Haitian Voodoo), or Macumba. On the continent, the traditional religious practices continue to exist, even with conversion to Christianity. Some people function in both capacities well, and others completely reject the African traditional practices for the exercise of the Christian faith.

Methodist missionaries to Africa also introduce reason, where the use of one's own way of perceiving God remains open. In other words, while the missionaries may have introduced a specific way of seeing God, or practicing Christianity, they also introduced openness. This openness allows for people to use their one humanity to understand God in their life. Using this opportunity helped in the process of translating the Gospel and other Christian literature in English, to indigenous languages of the people.

The other aspect of Wesleyanism is the introduction of the Bible, as God's "word." Confusing at first, it was difficult for Africans to perceive God's words as contained in a book with a few pages. Doesn't God still speak? What is God saying today? Are those words of the past remaining? Does God live in the now? These questions were perceived as blasphemous with the introduction of the bible to African people. However, the missionaries were more convincing than the questioners, and the Bible was accepted. Today, in many African countries where the United Methodist Church exists, these four aspects of the Wesleyan quadrilateral have been infused into the African culture and have made its way into the political culture.

American church culture was spread through the efforts of Black Church missionaries to Africa from various denominations. This American involvement in the church of Africa cannot be overlooked because even the Pentecostal movement that started at Azusa Street in Los Angeles in 1906-9 had impact on African church, regardless of the denomination.

African American Christianity started in the "invisible institutions" because during slavery, Africans, who were mostly enslaved people, did not mingle as equals with their Caucasian brothers and sisters. Although Black women maids took care of little white children, they were not allowed to worship in the same sanctuary as their white "masters" and "mistresses". However, they were given seating in the balcony of the church, if they went with their masters, and there was no participation for them in the church.

But the enslaved on the field, for which religious conversion had occurred, sometimes surreptitiously, saw the need to be "under their own vine and fig tree." Their status as enslaved people could not allow them the resources to construct large church buildings and institutions of worship. And furthermore, since they were not considered Christians, they were able to form groups to sneak or "steal away" to worship. The growth of the 'Invisible Institution' was to disguise their worship from their masters. The development of the Black church in that context, paved the way for the numerous Black Christian converts in the United States. As the institution became a church in the 1900s, this God-consciousness did not end in African American quarters, but spread to other parts of the world, including the Caribbean and Africa.

During the period of Puritan America (1620-1730), religious tolerance was not practiced by the colonialists or settlers, and religious freedom was not allowed to most others, such as Native Americans and African Americans. Some historians claim that the purpose of the coming of the puritans in the Massachusetts Bay area was because the reforms in the Church of England did not go far enough from its Roman Catholic heritage. But, while creating America for themselves, the Puritans virtually ignored the Native Americans and enslaved the Africans who had been brought to for enslavement.

Yet President Obama said, "This is America. And our commitment to religious freedom must be unshakeable. The principle that people of all faiths are welcome in this country and that they will not be treated differently by their government is essential to who were as a nation." This statement for the President of the United States paid tribute to the idea that America is historically a place of religious tolerance. Of course, whether George Washington and his nephew, Bushrod Washington, who was bent on establishing a colony of Black enslaved Americans in Africa, thought that project was a great idea. The Unites States of America became so because of the ideals of freedom that all the colonies, later states, shared in their historic existence.

For Africa, it is best to begin this around the Black Church Freedom Movement. This was a time of reevaluating interracial worship since Black and White worshippers were unequal in the church, and hence in the sight of God. From 1750 to 1861 it was common for Black Christians and White Christians to worship in the same congregations. But Black Christians did not necessarily enjoy any real equality or freedom in ecclesiastical status, especially because of the refusal for some white Christians to see that if "anyone is in Christ, the person is a new creature. Old things – including slave status – passed away, and everything becomes new."[1] They saw Native Americans and Black Christians as not "fit for the Kingdom," not based on their relationship to God, but on their ethnicity.

The white Christians who dominated the religious scene at the time held onto the notion that the American frontier defined American character. Wilmore notes that "the relationship pattern of whites and blacks in the household of God made it difficult for Americans to perceive that there was anything wrong with inequality in the household of Caesar."[2] However, little did they realize that American character was, and still is, defined by ethnicity?

Paul Cuffee was a member of a group of progressive Blacks in Massachusetts who were in contact with the Free African Society, forerunner of the African Methodist Episcopal Church started by Richard Allen, Absalom Jones, and others. Cuffee was a businessman, but was Christian, and his focus was on Africa. He undertook his own mission to Africa. That influence of Christianity on Cuffee fostered the idea of a black nationalistic consciousness, which sparked the zeal of African American believers to be interested in Africa, their ancestral homeland.

Looking to Africa was not simply for business but rather to "Christianize the land of their ancestors and to open up an administrative and communications network between churches for the promotion of Christian mission in both Africa and the Caribbean.[3] The ambition was that Africa would be the basis for spreading the faith to other parts of the Black world. With this zeal and with Liberia being still an idea, the place of enslaved Africans was still undefined in that they

---

[1] 2 Corinthians 5:17
[2] Gayraud Wilmore. *Black Religion and Black Radicalism: An Interpretation of the Religious History of African Americans.* (Maryknoll, New York: Orbis Books, 1998), 99.
[3] Wilmore, 126. Also Patrick Rael (Ed.). *African-American Activism before the Civil War: the Freedom Struggle in the Antebellum North.* (New York & London: Routledge, 2008), 212.

were not free in these United States, and they had no place in Africa or the Caribbean. This was dilemma for African Americans.

The idea that resulted in Sierra Leone and Liberia is something worth discussing because the connection to American religious history will become much clearer at the outset. The idea of freedom or liberation, i.e. the notion that resulted in what is Sierra Leone and Liberia in Africa, came from Samuel Hopkins, an American Congregationalist Pastor and former slave-owner from Newport, Rhode Island. This idea of Black emigration to Africa came around 1759.[4] The idea may or may not have evolved from the guilt and sin of owning fellow humans as property; he proposed to educate a few freed black people and send them back to Africa, since Africa's people had been "plundered."[5] This was the plan or idea that the American Colonization Society (ACS) – a group of former slave owners – chose to implement. Hence, we have the formation of Liberia in 1822, with independence from the ACS on July 26, 1847.

The men and women who started Liberia were all from the United States, although a few came later from the Caribbean. The presence and amount of freed blacks in the United States posed a threat to the American white society and the best solution was the creation of this country that became another "land of the free" or *Liber*, from Latin, connoting freedom. The capital city of Liberia is named after James Monroe, the fifth president of the United States who provided financial support to the idea of the American colonization Society. Liberia became a big help in the control of Black people movements in the United States, because even those African Americans who remained here, were basically denied connections to Africa. The influence of white American in Liberia's formation is from that point of slavery,

---

[4] Wilmore 127.
[5] Ibid.

to freedom, to Christianity, and to complete control of institutions and provisions.

The Black power movement in the United States impacted the Liberia Annual Conference in many unexpected ways. Although the Movement comprised various categories of Black pastors in the United States, it paved the way for the Methodist Church in Liberia to begin electing its own Bishops, from within its Conference or leadership.

The other factor was the African independence movement sweeping across the continent, with Ghana gaining its independence from Britain in 1957. The Civil Rights Movement and the African Independent Movement also worked with other progressive groups around the world to accomplish their goals.

The Black power movement in the United States gave inspiration to local ministers in Africa, and with many being trained at American universities and seminaries, the missionary Bishop, Prince A. Taylor, Jr., put in place plans for the Liberia Conference to elect its own Bishop, and then this will expand to Sierra Leone and the other countries.[6] Bishop Taylor's strategy was to foster local leadership of the church, leading to its total liberation or independence, at least, in the strategic leadership.[7] The conference continued to receive missionaries, both black and white, even when Bishop Nagbe was in office in the early seventies.

It is unclear whether Bishop Taylor himself was motivated by the African independent movement, the Civil Rights Movements, or whether he was visionary who did not want the church to be left behind in the historical developments of the country, and decided to let the Episcopacy be Liberian. It is not clear but Bishop Taylor's own

---

[6] Kenya, Zimbabwe, Angola, Congo, Nigeria, Cote d'Ivoire
[7] Some seminarians who served under Bishop Taylor were Samuel RE Dixon; Stephen T. Nagbe, Bennie D. Warner. Arthur Kulah, D. Seah Doe, Jacob N. Kartwe, Mark J. Richards.

writings, particularly his memoirs *The Life of My Years*, indicate his desire to let the Liberia Annual Conference be it independent Central Conference in United Methodism. Either way, Bishop Taylor's approach was to provide scholarship to Liberian United Methodist youths to study in the United States at graduate level and beyond, in seminary and other areas of study, especially where the church had need. Some of Bishop Taylor's students listed above returned to Liberia and held significant leadership roles in the church.

The US Constitution does not recognize God as the Supreme Being of the Country and despite the arguments that some Christian scholars have made that the USA was founded on 'Christian Principles,' more evidence show otherwise. The United States of America is not a Christian country, despite the zeal for religious freedom in its quest for being a nation-state.[8] The separation of church and state is defined in the US Constitution's First Amendment.[9] The influence of the church in America does not necessarily extend to government policies. This is one area of difference between Liberia and the United States.

Most of the founding parents of Liberia were Christians. Some were missionaries who also affiliated with the Methodist Church. Others in government may not have been in the leadership position, but they have been involved in both church and state. As such, it seems like Liberia was "founded on Christian principles." The Liberian church plays a key role in the decisions and policies of the government. It is hardly difficult to tell the difference between the church and the state because the presidents. Liberia is unique in that sense, from the United States. In 1977, Bishop Bennie D. Warner of the United Methodist Church was nominated and approved as Vice President to a Baptist Pastor, who was President of the Republic, Rev. William R. Tolbert, Jr. Many of President Tolbert's cabinets were Christians who

---

[8] John Fey. 147-168.
[9] "Congress shall make no laws . . ."

belonged to a Baptist, Methodist, Episcopalian, Lutheran, Catholic, Presbyterian, and other denominations. Christianity dominated socio-political climate. On Sundays, all businesses are closed, and the nothing happens, except church.

Missionaries of African descent who travelled to Liberia had two reasons at the back of their minds: to spread the Gospel of Jesus and the get away from the Jim Crow laws and the racism that characterized American society. The role of the missionaries to Liberia was in developing and improving the chance for local leadership. One of the benefits of missionaries in this category is they offered an alternative lifestyle and belief with the settlers (some of whom were missionaries), and later with the indigenous Liberians.

The main argument of Liberia's historiography – the focus on native and settlers – is more evident in the late 20th century with prevailing cultural and religious difference. Native revolts continued, especially between the Settlers and the Kaw people, including the Bassa, Grebo, and Kru specifically. The simple point of indignation on the part of the indigenous people toward the settlers was that the latter exhibited a superior attitude and an elitist mentality. Despite such climate of disharmony, and in some cases danger, mission efforts were not deterred or discouraged. It continued from with force, because the missionaries felt like they were the hope that could bring about harmony between the indigenous peoples and the Settlers.

In the 1900s, American religious influence continued to spread throughout Liberia by the tireless and concerted efforts of the African American missionaries and their Caucasian counterparts. The Methodist Episcopal Church, for example, selected Caucasian bishops for Liberia and Africa. Later in the history of the church, the elected Liberians for Liberia. The African Methodist Episcopal Church also had its first local resident Bishop in 1908. Rev. William H. Heard and his wife spent 12 years. It is important to mention that Bishop and

Mrs. Heard attempted to plant schools that could produce an intelligent citizenry and tools for self-empowerment.[10]

The rise of African American mission work draws on the historical experiences of liberation and emancipation. The settlers and the missionaries felt like they were being granted equality under the law in Liberia. Liberia's name underscored the desire for liberation or freedom from thralldom. African Americans, after slaver was over, lost their basic human rights to organized hate groups that terrorized black Americans, before, during, and after Reconstruction (1863-1877).

The history of early Methodism in Africa continues today where the ongoing Africa and America relations continue. The black American missionaries in Africa, who worked specifically with the indigenous people, tend to have the most impact on that ethnic group. For example, the mainline denominations such as the Baptist, Episcopalian, Methodist, Lutheran, and Catholic whose missionaries worked along the coast with the Bassa, Kru, Grebo, etc. because these groups are coastal peoples, successfully converted them. Here is an example of a missionary of African American descent who worked in Liberia, and the positive impact she is remembered for. Missionary, particularly African American women, caught on in the 20th century. Although there is paucity on their contributions, there are some materials and sources from which researchers can work.

The Methodist Episcopal Church 'recruited a Black woman as missionary, Anna Hall. She was 36 years old and worked specifically with the Garraway Mission and near Harper. She was born and raised in Georgia, and completed a deaconess training in Boston,

---

[10] H. T. Kealing. "A General Conference Letter to Theophilus," *The AME Review*, Vol XXV, #1 (July 1908, 68-69. See also W. H. Heard, "A Parting Word," *AME Review,* Vol. XXV, #1, (July 1908), 68-69.

which qualified her to be consecrated with assignment to Liberia.[11] Ms. Hall's influence extended to many women from the Cape Palmas, Maryland area, who played (and still play) key leadership role in the Liberia Annual Conference. From her funeral bulletin, Ms. Hall spent 25 years in Liberia as missionary. Based on her commitment and dedication to Liberia, Presented William VS Tubman, a Methodist, awarded her Knight Commander of the Liberian Humane Order, and invited her to the presidential inauguration in 1956.[12] Ms. Hall had one significant motto: "Not four ourselves but for others."[13]

The history of the United States begins in a desire – one in which the freedom of protestant worship could be unhampered, and the need to be free not under a monarchy. Religious "pilgrims" who settled in the USA, such as the Puritans, were desirous of having a place where they could worship God freely, and have their stamp placed on the religious culture of this new society. The Pilgrims who landed on Plymouth Rock in 1620 also felt it was their God-given right to "Christianize" the Native Americans here, and referred to them as "heathens" or "uncivilized" people. The history is such that the indigenous people who were being targeted for Christianity and civilization were considered, in the minds of the pilgrims, as such, and it was their (pilgrims') responsibility to make sure that Christianity and civilization prevailed in the lives of Native Americans.

Therefore, upon arrival on this continent, the pilgrims established various churches throughout. And churches are still being built. The church was to appease the native people and to show to them that they were sinners, and only God would save them. The American

---

[11] Emma. W. Strother. "Black Women in United Methodism," General Board of Global Ministries, n.d.; also "Funeral Service Bulletin of Ms. Anna E. Hall," *Central Methodist Church*, (Atlanta, Georgia, March 1964).
[12] "Miss Anna Hall Dies, Outstanding Citizen," *Atlanta Daily World*, Sunday, March 8, 1964.
[13] Funeral Service Bulletin of Ms. Anna E. Hall, March 9, 1964.

society has continued to be a church country. All the denominations of Christianity are now represented in the United States.

This connection is unique because Liberia is the only country in Africa where Americanism or western Christian culture still dominates. The connection between both countries started with the end of slavery, and the desire for the former slave holders to get rid of their former slaves, and others who had not been enslaved. Following slavery, there were many freed black people, who could outnumber whites in some cities and towns. The scheme to send freed blacks back to Africa is what resulted into Liberia. And there was a specific quest – a place or environment to worship God freely, and the absence of a political monarchy. The native Americans bore the brunt of that decision, but it also affected the entire world. The desire to create Christendom helped the American brand of Christianity reach Africa. In Liberia, the experiment of establishing a country for people who were enslaved in America, albeit from Africa, was a way out. It was a way out of slavery and the issue of massive freed black people at the time.

The religious history of the United States which began with European Settlers was transported nearly 200 years later to Liberia. As indicated in this work, the earliest settlements for Liberia started 1820, which will make it exactly 200 years when the English Pilgrim settlers arrived in Massachusetts. While these English pilgrims were motivated by the protestant faith, the Liberian settlers were not simply motivated by faith. They were motivated by the notion of emancipation, freedom, liberation, and salvation for those they would encounter. Unlike the English pilgrims in the United States, the Settlers from the United States were not only seeking a place for peace, but also a place they could call home. Elijah Johnson, one of the Settlers, upon reaching Liberia, and amidst the commotion that erupted among them, said, "For two hundred years I have been searching for a home.

Here [Liberia] I have found one, and here I shall remain."[14] A great majority of the Settlers to Liberia were Protestants who had affiliations with the Baptist, Episcopal, Lutheran, Methodist, or Presbyterian churches. Now, they could practice in peace.

When the Settlers settled in Liberia, their goal was to build a nation and several churches, but the goal was to have the freedom to worship, regardless of the challenges or obstacles. Some settlers felt they had a God-given right to convert indigenous Africans to Christianity at any cost. Freedom because the expression, hence the name Liberia, - free land of liberty. The Settlers built churches just like the American pilgrims. Their efforts were on building a state, and building church

Although Liberian theology has embraced a neo-Pentecostal aspect, scholars and historians still debate whether Liberia is a "Christian" nation. Even though it was established on "Christian principles," it is not acceptable to all that Liberia is exclusively a Christian nation, like Iran, the Islamic State, or Saudi Arabia. Historians argue over who has more influence – Christianity or Islam or indigenous religions. But a closer look at the founding fathers and mothers of Liberia, they were affiliated with various denominations before they came. Of course, one will use what one is born into. So, the Settlers resorted to their Christian beliefs and attitudes in everything they did. It was with such attitudes and beliefs that they interacted with indigenous peoples, Europeans, and others. Recognition of the connection between Liberian religious history and American religious history also lies in the rise and fall of Christian diversity and the hope that humanity will coexist peacefully.

The United Methodist Church in Liberia is the church's oldest mission field, but it is the least developed. Also, people who write history

---

[14] A. Doris Banks Henries. *Liberia: History of the First African Republic*. (London: Macmillan Publishers, 1960), 17.

of the Church refer to the Liberia Conference as coming to existence in 1833. These two facts are significant to this book because I intend to discuss the development issue, and to dispel the notion that the church started in 1833.

The first two Bishops of the United Methodist Church in Liberia are Francis Burns, and John Wright Roberts. They were also among the first Blacks to be elected to the Episcopacy in the Church. Although, due to paucity of information on their contributions to the church in Liberia, they have not been given the recognition they deserve, they are among the Pioneers of the Church in Liberia, as well as Pioneers in the creation of what is now Liberia. This article provides information on these two giants of the Church in Liberia and explores their historical significance to Liberia.

Methodism in Liberia started with the arrival of the Settlers. Even though most Methodist Church historians recognize the arrival to Liberia of Melvin Cox in 1833, as the beginning of Methodism in Liberia, he was not the first to introduce Methodism to the nation in waiting. The fact that he was the first Caucasian Methodist Missionary to Liberia, does not negate the efforts of Daniel Cooker, (later moved to Sierra Leone), an African Methodist Episcopal Church Missionary, along with several of the people who arrived on that first load of ship from the United States. Among them were Elijah Johnson, Beverley Wilson, Hilary Teague, Joseph Roberts, (Liberia's first President), John Wright Roberts (Second Liberian Methodist Bishop, and brother of JJ Roberts), and Henry Roberts, the other brother who was a Physician. These were men, and their wives, were not just pioneers in nation building, but also in church building. Despite our opinion of them as individuals, these were the original Methodists from which all Methodists spread in Africa.

Since then, the syndrome of dependency and the cultivation of a culture of dependency have characterized the nature and scope of the church. However, before the Settlers or Americo-Liberians were solidly in place, we cannot forget that the natives of the Grain Coast, were not only Africanists, but had experienced Christianity from other Europeans who were traders, along the Coast of West Africa.

The missionaries discussed here also share similar characteristics with the Settlers in terms of language and understanding. Each person will be mentioned where necessary. It is possible that these men and their families, upon reaching Africa, Liberia, to be exact, felt like the proverbial ball was in their courts. They had to face life on their own, build a society that was of their own design, and create churches that represented their socio-political mindset. The same United States where they had been enslaved, had to give them "language," "culture" and other aspects of being humans. The feeling of superiority based on skin or complexion was a big part of the Settlers' language and culture. The introduction of exclusive fraternities such as the Masons, the UBFs, and other forms of secret engagements, developed out of the need for the Settlers to establish their own culture. The dilemma they faced, however, was that they could not completely be Americans again, and they did not willingly embrace their indigenous lifestyles, perhaps because for them, the latter was inferior. Hence, the idea of superiority in the minds of the Settlers at that time! In all these lived experiences, the Settlers and the indigenous Liberians managed to coexist, under written laws and unwritten rules of engagement, and with the Settlers in control. All the Americo-Liberian men discussed here were born outside of Liberia and immigrated to Liberia to become one of the pioneers of Methodism.

5

METHODIST INDIGENOUS BISHOPS IN AFRICA SINCE 1964

The first indigenous African Bishop of the Methodist Church did not come from Liberia, even though Liberia is the oldest mission conference. He came from Zimbabwe, a mission conference that grew out of the Liberia Annual Conference. However, Francis Burns and John Wright Roberts, the first two Black bishops of Methodism, were founding members of the Libera Annual Conference in 1834, and they were also African American men who settled in Liberia.

The Methodist episcopacy in Liberia changed forever in 1965. Since then, the Church has elected Bishops who were born and raised in Liberia, and who belong to indigenous Liberian citizenry. What led to this dramatic change? What was the status of the Episcopacy in Liberia prior to 1965? These two questions form the basis of this short discussion on Methodism in Liberia.

In 1965, when most of Africa was gaining independence and when the civil rights movement had picked up enough steam to threaten the American social fabric, all institutions concerned or connected to this great power trembled. The only solution was to provide opportunities in self-determination, independence, and self-control. In this connection, the need for a local Liberian Bishop who was of Liberian heritage, was advanced, by the then missionary bishop of the church.

The Methodist Church in Liberia experienced its Episcopal independence in 1965. No woman has been elected Bishop of the Conference since its establishment in 1834. The following men have been elected bishop: Stephen Trowen Nagbe, Sr., Bennie DeQuincy Warner; Arthur Flumo Kulah; John Innis; and Samuel Quire. Profiles are available for Bishops Nagbe, Warner, and Kulah. For Bishops Innis and Quire, no profiles are available because their respective leadership were ethically controversial, and to publish on their contributions, if any, to Methodism as a whole, is questionable.

Stephen Trowen Nagbe, Sr.
1965-1972

In 1965, Stephen Trowen Nagbe was elected in Harper, Mar County, as the first indigenous person to be Bishop of the Methodist Church in Liberia. It was a historic triumph for the conference because throughout, or at least since the episcopacy of William Taylor, the need for local leadership had been the focal point. Nagbe's election was the beginning of that dream becoming a reality.

In 1964, the General Conference gave Liberian United Methodists two options. One option was to become an autonomous church/conference; or to form a Methodist Conference with the right to elect its own bishops. Liberia opted for the latter, and Bishop Stephen Trowen Nagbe, Sr. was elected on the second ballot in Cape Palmas, Maryland County, Liberia. The information focuses on Bishop Nagbe's profile.

His episcopacy was historic because it opened doors for the Liberia Annual Conference to be independent in its leadership, but not in its missions. His election proved that Liberians were able to run the affairs of the church. He died in 1972.

Bennie DeQuincy Warner
1972-1980

In 1973 following Nagbe's unexpected death from cancer, Bishop Bennie DeQuincy Warner became his successor. Bishop Warner was elected in Buchanan, Grand Bassa County, at the First UMC, on Church Street. His tenure was progressive in that he became Vice President of Liberia under President Tolbert, a Baptist minister.

Many believed President Tolbert selected Bishop Warner as his vice President because the Bishop was very outspoken. For example, Bishop Warner was critical of a Gambling Bill passed by the Liberian legislature. In one sermon he preached on Camphor Mission, he expressed disappointment in the legislature for passing such a Bill. The Bishop justified his criticism of the bill with a scripture: "Wealth from gambling quickly disappears, but wealth from hard work remains."[1] The Bishop was also critical of the Government for its export policies, when Liberia was expelled from exporting coffee to the world market, because Liberian merchants were sending rocks, instead of coffee, in export bags to the world market.

While serving as bishop of the United Methodist Conference of Liberia, Warner was selected by President William R. Tolbert Jr. to serve as Vice President, succeeding Vice President James Edward These and many other criticisms were loud, and so when James E. Green, Tolbert's second Vice President died, the Bishop was nominated. At his inauguration as Vice President, Bishop Warner remained to his principles, by identifying the problems of Liberia, speaking on the theme: "What is wrong with Liberia is us." Bishop Warner was Vice President and Bishop, both full-time jobs. Greene. Green died in late 1977, but Warner was nominated and inaugurated in 1978.

---

[1] Proverbs 13:6

In 1980, Liberia had a coup that deposed the Tolbert regime. Vice President and Bishop Bennie Warner had travelled to the United States for a Conference. Although Tolbert was killed in the coup, Bishop Warner survived, and is alive to "tell the story." Many Liberians felt that he was truly a "Man of God," because he left Liberia less than five days before the coup. The Church was left without a Bishop because Warner could not return to Liberia after the military leaders and politicians in power threatened to kill him if he did return. He did not.

Arthur Flumo Kulah
1980-2000

As the First United Methodist Church in Monrovia, Bishop Arthur Flumo Kulah was elected to succeed Bishop Warner. Bishop Kulah, a relatively humble and God-fearing man, served in that capacity until his retirement in 2000. Arthur F. Kulah, son of Saye and Zonpu Kulah, was born in Kanyea, a small village in rural Liberia, on October 5, 1936. As the eldest son of a tribal chief, he spent his early years, together with the rest of the family, in farming and other rural activities. While attending Cuttington College and Divinity School, Arthur was also pastor of First Church in Suakoko. He then became superintendent of the Gbarnga District.

He was ordained Elder by Bishop S. Trowen Nagbe, the first indigenous bishop, and later joined the Liberia Annual Conference in 1968. Kulah continued his formal education at St. Paul School of Theology, from where he obtained a Master of Religious Education (M.R.E.) in 1970. He returned to Liberia and was appointed Director of Christian Education, and Dean of Gbarnga School of Theology. He again went to the United States to receive both a M.Div. (1978) and a D.Min. (1980) from Wesley Theological Seminary. During 1978- 79, he was Director of the Conference Course of Study.

A few months after he returned to his responsibilities at the Gbarnga School of Theology, the Liberia Central Conference elected Arthur F. Kulah to the episcopacy. He was consecrated in Miller McAllister United Methodist Church on December 7, 1980. With the formation of the West Africa Central Conference, Bishop Kulah was assigned to the Liberia Area. His successor, John G. Innis, became bishop in 2000.

6

METHODIST MISSION TARGETS &
THE BASSA PEOPLE SINCE 1900

The Bassa People of Liberia

This chapter introduces Bassa people in Liberia as a microcosm for mission work among indigenous peoples in Africa. The Bassa people in Liberia are predominantly Christians and their involvement in touch related environments expand wide and far. With respect to the Methodists in Liberia, the Bassa people are a significant component of Methodism in this country. The fact that the entire indigenous Bassa population is Christian does mean success in mission. This success does not undermine the Bassa culture. The focus is on the Bassa people and how Christianity reached them in the 1900s and since then. The discussion extends to translation of materials for use in Bassa churches, such as the Apostles' Creed, and the Lord's Prayer.

The bishops, who served the African Conferences – whether as missionary or "regular" bishops - demonstrate that the indigenous people were, and still are mission targets. The Methodist Church in Africa could not develop only with the missionaries and the Settlers from the United States. The indigenous involvement in Christianity is a history that needs to be written. Without the indigenous peoples, there would be no Church growth.

Knowing this, those mainline denominations who wished to extend their version of the Christian faith in Africa, had to target indigenous peoples. In Liberia, the Kwa people are mostly people who live near to coastal areas of the country, except for the Vai, who belong to the Mande group, and are in Grand Cape Mount County[1]. The Bassa people, as a microcosm of the Kwa group, converted to Christianity, and this conversion can be considered a success of Mission enterprise among indigenous African peoples.

To delve deeply into the Bassa people and their conversion to Christianity, it is important to begin with a background on the Bassa people. The Bassa people in Liberia are not the same Bassa people found in Cameroon, Cote d'Ivoire, Nigeria, or Ghana or any other parts of Africa. Although all the Bassa peoples on the continent of Africa have a common origin, it is important to state here that, in this work, and the Bassa people of Liberia are the focus of this discussion, relative to the success of Missionary enterprise of the Methodist Church.

The basic worldview of Bassa people is summarized in three aspects: family; traditional institutions and society; and the diviners or healers. These three aspects shaped how life used to be prior to the interaction and arrival of Europeans and Settlers. The three aspects of this worldview are related intricately, yet, each exercises its own authority on society.

A distinctive element of the Kwa, along with the people listed above, is that they called the region that became Liberia their home prior to 1820. As early as 1365, European traders, along with their hosts, built settlements at sites near Petit Dieppe (now Buchanan) and Grand Dieppe (Cestos River/Rivercess). The Europeans abandoned the sites

---

[1] Linguists divide Liberian indigenous peoples into three distinct groups: the Mel, the Mande, and the Kwa. The Kwa people mostly live along the coastal areas, and include, Bassa, Belle, Dey, Grebo, Jabo, Krahn, Kru, and Sapo. The Mel People include the Gola and the Kissi. The Mande include the Dan (Gio), Maa (Mano), Mandingo, Kpelle, Lorma, and Vai.

around, for the southern tip of Africa, using the south western coastal areas. They abandoned the sites in 1413.[2] By the middle of the 15th century A.D., Europeans and Bassa people were exchanging goods and services. Another trade center was built in Newcess, Grand Bassa County.[3]

Missionaries discouraged the use of Bassa people's diviners or herbalists, sometimes called medicine men or women, from teaching Bassa beliefs, and practicing traditional healing. As a result, two groups of healers emerged among the Bassa people: the "*Hwiohn*" and "*Hwe-nyon*." The *Hwion* is considered the diviner who uses herbs to heal the sick and afflicted, and he or she could function in the church. The *Hwe-nyon* is considered the diviner who uses herbs to do evil or harm. This person will never be welcomed in the church. While people see the former diviner as generally good, they see the latter as wicked, fearful, and therefore evil. However, both diviners can do what the other one does. One could be considered sacred, and the other secular, despite the similarity in their functions.

While these two personalities or categories of Bassa spiritualists are different, both function mainly in the use of indigenous proverbs, sayings, or parables, some of which may apply to Christian theology or Christian practice. Even among indigenous liturgies such as naming of child or children, and the expressions of joy when a child graduates from the indigenous *maagba* or *gaagba*, Christian understanding of joy is not different. But such teachings were discouraged and are still discouraged in some sectors of African theology, as incompatible with the church. Here, it must be understood that we are talking about the church, not God.

Over the last century, more Bassa churches have been built. This increase is a result of church planting efforts by missionaries and their

---

[2] William Siegmann. *Ethnographic Survey of Southeastern Liberia: Report on the Bassa.* (Robertsport, Liberia: Tubman Center of African Culture, 1969), 7.
[3] Siegmann, 6.

cohorts. Today, the churches have developed, or are developing a more local theology and being more indigenous, instead of Eurocentric or American. Bassa churches also are becoming more spontaneous with less or no overseas connection. Furthermore, they are becoming more Pentecostal in nature and scope.

An insight into Bassa people's history can provide some insight into Native people as mission targets. There are approximately one million Bassa people living in Liberia and in exile. Bassa homeland stretches from the Atlantic Ocean (southern) to the nearly three hundred, fifty miles into the interior (northern/northeastern). Bassa Counties[4] and communities exist in all of Liberia's counties.[5] Each of the Bassa counties, apart from Margibi, lies along the Atlantic coast, and extends further into the interior of Liberia, up to 300 miles, calculating from the coast.

Christianity
among the Bassa people

During this era of colonization, commerce, and Christianity, European and American – both Black and White – missionaries saw the need to spread the Gospel to all peoples around the globe. They were fulfilling "The Great Commission" of Matthew 28:18-21, where Jesus admonished the Disciples to "Go into the world, making disciples, and baptizing them in the name of the Father, the Son, and the Holy Spirit." Missionaries – both Black and White – traveling to Africa "winning souls for Christ," were introducing their brand of

---

[4] In Liberia, a county is a political division. Each county (Grand Bassa, Rivercess, Margibi, and Montserrado) hosts native peoples and Americo-Liberians. Native people are majority.

[5] The counties listed here are predominantly Bassa, apart from Montserrado, where there is more diversity, especially in Monrovia. The descriptions I mention above specifically refer to Grand Bassa County and Rivercess, not Margibi and Montserrado. There are 15 counties in Liberia.

Christianity on the local African population they met. But they also wanted the message to belong to the new converts.

Chinua Achebe talks about this phenomenon of conversion in his classic, *Things Fall Apart*[6] (1959). African converts did not simply accept the teachings of the missionaries because they had nothing to fall back on, or because they had no experience with the Divine. Rather, Africans were embracing a reality that had existed among them all along – the reality of a Supreme Being, a monotheistic concept, which had not been codified in books or on tablets, but was experienced in the day-to-day life of people. When missionaries introduced the same concept, albeit in a different fashion, African converts felt at home, and they also wanted to be participants, not spectators on this new "theological sporting complex."

By the 1900s, the Settlers started penetrating interior areas in Liberia to know for themselves what was there. But first, accounts of two British men, Benjamin JK Anderson, and Graham Greene, gave the Settlers some insight into the people living beyond the Du River. For his part, Anderson did not simply journey through the Bassa land; he penetrated all interior Liberia. Greene, for his part, went from Monrovia, to Kakata to Bassa, to Kokoyah, Bong, and back to Monrovia, passing by numerous villages and towns. These two men experienced the generosity of the indigenous Liberians, who were just becoming citizens of Liberia. Missionaries of the Methodist, Baptist, and other some other churches such as the Lutherans, the Pentecostals, ventured beyond Monrovia, Buchanan, and Greenville, the cities, to reach indigenous populations, during this era.

History of the Settlers' involvement in Liberia's church history begins with the *Rev. Lott Carey*, (Baptist), 1821–1828, a Baptist missionary to Liberia. It is unclear whether he specifically worked with Bassa people. *Rev. Daniel Coker*, a founding member of the Free African Society, represented what became the African Methodist Episcopal (AME)

---

[6] Chinua Achebe. *Things Fall Apart*. New York: Fawcett Books, 1959.

Church in 1822. He was the chaplain for the group of Settlers arriving that year. It is unlikely that he spent any time with Bassa people.

When the *Basel Mission* opened in 1828, they adopted a Bassa youth, *Jacob Vambrum*, who they trained and converted. *Vambrum* was probably the first indigenous Bassa person to be converted to Christianity. How his conversion came about is unclear. He was educated by the missionaries from the Basel Christian Mission or Switzerland in Sierra Leone and returned to Liberia to work among the Bassa people. The Basel mission relocated to Sierra Leone after a year's operations in Liberia.

The Presbyterian Church in America sent Rev. *John B. Pinney* to Liberia in 1833, with specific instructions to work with "the aborigines, and only incidentally for the colonialists."[7] The instruction to work with "aborigines" is clear, but there is little evidence he worked with the Bassa people.

Melville Cox, the first Methodist Episcopal Church missionary to Liberia, arrived in 1833. His appeal to the Board of Missions is now the slogan for mission work in the Methodist Church: "Although ten thousand may fall, let Africa never be given up."[8] He lived for three months in Liberia before he died. He also laid the groundwork for the Church by purchasing land to build school, church, and clinic, among others. During his time in Liberia, he and John B. Pinney of the Presbyterian Church shared the same house.

With respect to the Methodist Church among the Bassa people, a people's mass conversion movement developed in the early 1920s in the interior areas of Bassa. Ministers from the Methodist Episcopal

---

[7] Nassau, Rev. R. H. *Historical Sketch of the Missions in Africa, under the care of the Board of Foreign Missions of the Presbyterian Church.* (Philadelphia: Woman's Foreign Missionary Society of the Presbyterian Church, 1881), 6. The colonialists represent the Settlers or Americo-Liberians, in current expressions.

[8] Quoted in Gresham's work on Cox, 123.

Church (MEC) were inspired by God to undertake this movement[9]. The MEC ministers were Bassa men who were mentored or trained by Americo-Liberians in the so-called "civilized" MECs along the coasts of Buchanan and Monrovia.

James Deputie, an African-American leader in the MEC, mentored Rev. Henry Neor, a Bassa man. Henry Neor, an AME minister, and Bassa, evangelized his people in the 1900s. Neor takes credit for being the first Bassa minister to "speak in tongues, tremble during prayer, and divine healing."[10] Neor introduced the "holy water and oil." The water and oil continue to be important examples of spiritual power, especially in the independent churches and Prayer Bands.[11] People still venerate Neor, especially among the elderly, who usually mention him in prayers and sermons. Neor is the role model for Bassa Christianity and the Holy Spirit. Through Rev. Neor's preaching, George Goosa Dean was converted.

George Zeehdyu Goosa Dean started his ministry after he woke up from a week in a trance. While in trance, someone gave him some "tickets" and requested that he distribute the "tickets" among the people. For him, the dream represented God's calling on his life, and he started ministering to Bassa people. The "tickets" were pumpkin seeds.[12] Also from the dream, Goosa Dean obtained special powers for healing, prophecy, like traditional Bassa diviners. For his powers, Dean relied solely on the Holy Ghost. Goosa Dean felt this dream, "Gave him power to spread the Gospel of Jesus to Bassa people. He

---

[9] MEC = Methodist Episcopal Church, forerunner of the United Methodist Church.
[10] Rev. J. C. Early, 1998.
[11] Prayer Band is popular among women groups in Bassa churches. Their main purpose is to meet periodically to fast and pray for everything. They hold special Prayer conferences, which last between one to two weeks. They also "dry fast" daily during these conferences.
[12] Pumpkin seeds are representation of the "Spirit." Depending on its application or purpose, it may be a good spirit or bad spirit. In this case, it was a good Zuwheenwheen (Holy Spirit), literally, "Clean Spirit." Since the pumpkin seeds were good spirits, each seed grew into a church.

got extra-spiritual powers, like a person who was dealing.[13] But he used them for the Holy Ghost. Even when the Old Man came to town, people noticed him because some would meet him crying, sometimes stripping them, and ready to change, ready to repent."[14]

Dean preached by explaining the basics of the Christian message. He would repeat a person's name three times, and on the fourth time, the person was cleansed. Dean performed these spiritual activities under the Methodist Episcopal Church. The MEC, which later became the United Methodist Church (UMC), had Americo-Liberian leaders. The Church leaders refused to recognize or accept Goosa Dean's gifts and graces, denying him the opportunity to ordain as a minister. If he wanted to baptize the native Bassa converts, he had to with the converts at Buchanan. This was where the baptisms took place. A year or two later, Dean refused to travel to Buchanan for baptism, and baptized his converts himself in places in the interior that he visited. Even though the Church refused to recognize him, Dean continued doing ministry.

The Church took Dean to court for doing ministry without ordination or proper license. The case was pending. Before rendering the decision, the presiding judge died. His death, the night before had the chance to render his decision, became a sacred intervention. Leaders in the MEC took this as a sign that God did not want them to sabotage or stop Dean's work. They dropped the case and before long, they gave Dean his ordination.[15] Dean and the Bassa converts remained in the MEC for nearly fifteen years. But various conflicts, including class consciousness, finances, and integrity, among others, persisted, developing mistrust on both sides.

---

[13] "Dealing" is a term generally associated with engaging in African traditional herbs or science. A diviner may also be "dealing."
[14] J. C. Early. *Memoirs of JC Early: The St. John River District UMC in Perspective*. (Atlanta, Georgia: Unpublished Manuscript), 6.
[15] Early, 1998.

In 1946, a Liberian court split the MEC District in two, giving Bassa native Methodists their own district, and the Americo-Liberian Methodists their own district: the Bassa "A" (Americo-Liberian) District, and the Bassa "B" District (native Bassa speakers). But by 1975, the Bassa Methodists changed their district to St. John River District, since "B" represented an inferior class status. This new name helped them feel total liberation from "bondage."

In 1944, *Sam Samuels* a MEC Pastor, in what is now the St. John River District, UMC, experienced the fruit of the Holy Spirit. Methodists did not get "caught up in the spirit." Rev. Samuels advocated the confession of sins and the renunciation of traditional healing. He claimed to speak as the Holy Spirit directed him. He felt called by God to pass on the Holy Spirit to his town's people and family. Upon leaving the MEC, Samuels formed fellowship with Kru Pentecostals in Monrovia: the Pentecostal Assemblies of the World (PAW) Church. This union was short lived mainly because both Bassa and Kru Christians could not find common approaches to maintain their unity.

But besides Samuels, other native Bassa Christians were experiencing the Holy Spirit. Soon, the Holy Spirit fever gripped Bassa Christians like fire on dry leaves. Meanwhile, three surrounding Bassa villages experienced the same spirit phenomenon, when the pillar of fire appeared in the sky at midpoint. The three Bassa villages, (still existing), include: *Josay Glay ble, Gbo-yogaa ble*, and *Neeya-peh ble*.[16] When the pillar of fire disappeared, villagers in the three were swamped in "the spirit."

When Samuels explained this unusual happening to Goosa Dean, the latter dismissed him. Even though Dean himself came from similar background, he failed to recognize Samuels' spiritual gifts. Instead, he reported Samuels to Rev. W. P. L. Brumskine, the Americo-

---

[16] "*Ble* is the Bassa word for town or village.

Liberian Superintendent at the time. Superintendent Brumskine acknowledged the power of the Holy Ghost, drawing a parallel of Samuels' experience to the Apostles in Acts 2, essentially admitting that Samuels did no wrong. Yet, he approved Samuels and his followers leaving the MEC.[17]

Between 1949 and 1950, Bassa men and women residing in cities like Buchanan and Monrovia, returned to their native homes to fulfill the rite of passage in the Maagba (women) and Gaagba (men). Reasons for this increase remain unclear. Perhaps, it was difficult for people in some areas of Bassaland[18] to get a government job unless they were graduates of either school. This was a strange happening in these areas. Most powerful ex-pupils from these schools also penetrated the Church, and the Americo-Liberian Methodists saw this as opportunity to control of the native Methodists again. But the Bassa Methodists designed another strategy to free themselves from their brothers' control by getting initiated in the Maagba or Gaagba. Court actions did not threaten the Bassa Methodists any longer.

Translation & Indigenous Practical Theology

Translation of Christian literature such as the Bible, the Apostle Creeds, and Hymns into indigenous Bassa, made it easier for Bassa people to feel accepted, and to experience a sense of belonging to this Christian idea. Translation is the key instrument of proselytizing among the Bassa that the missionaries used. It started with not simply the Methodists who were Bassa speaking, but with other Bassa Christians. The Bassa people's conversion to Christianity opened the way for Bassa people to be literate in their indigenous

---

[17] Early, 1998.
[18] Bassa County has several districts. The districts in this case were #3, #5, and Rivercess.

language, through translation of western Christian literature to indigenous Bassa.

One of the greatest concerns of Christian missionaries as they reached Liberia and tried to convert Bassa People to Christianity was ensuring that the message of the Gospel of Christ Jesus reached the people. As a result, there have been several mission and local efforts at translating the message from English to the indigenous Bassa. Ever since the late 19th century when Christian missionaries reached Liberia to convert Bassa people to Christianity, ensuring that the gospel message reached Bassa people, was of immediate concern, as a result, there have been efforts – both from the missionaries and local leaders – at translating the message of the gospel to indigenous tongues. These efforts started with shorter scriptures such as Psalm 23, the Lord's Prayer, and the Apostle's Creed, among others. Today, the entire Bible and several hymns have been translated to Bassa.

This chapter looks at the translated version of the Apostles' Creed, and what have been the impact of this translation to Bassa people, and their understanding of the Christian faith. Has the translation of the Apostle's Creed given Bassa people any "value" in the wider Christian scheme of things, or by this translation, is there a new creed that they recite? These are the two questions that drive the discussion of this research.

Preliminary findings reveal that the current recitation of the Apostle's Creed in Bassa is more aligned to the Ancient African creed, than it is with the English, the language of the current translation. If this finding holds throughout, it is fair to say then that the Bassa version of the creed speaks more to what the creed meant to accomplish in Christians worldwide, than what the English missionaries provided. It is also fair to propose that the recited Bassa version should be considered the official Creed for Bassa people, without using its English equivalent in the liturgy.

The Apostle's Creed is significant in the liturgy of Christianity. Wherever there is a Christian Church, there is the possibility that the Apostle Creed is part of their liturgy or has been incorporated in their worship experience, either in the Confessions or other church-specific documents. In other words, the Apostles' Creed is so important in Christian liturgy, it is hard to ignore because it forms the basis of understanding of what it means to be a Christian, along with the Nicene and Athanasian Creeds. Bassa Christians in Liberia – whether in the Methodist Church; Catholic Church, Episcopal Church, Baptist, or African Methodist Church – subscribe to the understanding of the Apostles' Creed, and as such, they have translated the Creed so that non-English speaking Bassa Christians can participate in the liturgy of the said church. Translation of the Apostles' Creed did not happen overnight among the Bassa Christians in Liberia. One can attribute the English translation of the creed, from which the Bassa version has developed, to the early 1800s, when missionaries started working among the people.

William Crocker of the Baptist denomination was one of the first missionaries, who, when working with the Bassa People decided to have translate the Bassa language in English and vice versa, so his converts could be able to communicate in both Bassa and English. Crocker wanted his 'students' to be able to read the Bible in both English and Bassa. Prior to Crocker's coming, the Bass People had their own writing system. What Crocker and others who followed him later up to the 20th century did, was to use the original *vha-chede*, (name of the traditional writing system), and equated the sounds of the language to the Latin version.

There is no doubt that what Crocker and other later translators did was to adopt the Church of English version of Creed published in 1662 in the *Book of Common Prayer*. Of the Church of English and its antecedent denomination, the Anglican and Episcopal, it was the Methodist church that made tremendous inroads among the Bassa

People. Even though the Baptist Church was one of the first denominations to introduce Christianity to the people, the Methodist has made tremendous inroads among the Bassa people. In fact, most of the Bassa Independent Churches that developed between 1959 and the early 1960s were disgruntled former Bassa Methodist Christians.

The Apostles' Creed reached Bassa Christians through the Methodist Church. The Methodist and the Lutherans are two of the mainline denominations that focused their mission activities in rural areas of the country. The other mainline churches such as the Baptists, Presbyterians, Episcopalians, Catholics, and Seven Day Adventists, among others, focused their mission with the city dwellers, many of whom were indigenous, but mainly Settlers.[19] The Bassa People adopted Methodism because Methodism had a much stronger organization and its willingness to decentralize ecclesial leadership. Political decentralization of is in line with Bassa cultural experience. Villages and towns in Bassa 'country' are much smaller in size and population compared to the Kpelle, for example, because the Bassa People like their leadership decentralized. Decentralization allows each person to be his/her boss.

The Creed has also created among Bassa Christians decentralization: an individual one, in which each person has a right and privilege to affirm God in their perspective. Although the Creed is recited in a public confession setting in the church, it places everyone *in media res,* during things. As used here, in media res, refers to the context in which the Creedal recitation by a Bassa Christian, placing him/her during thousands of other Christians who recite or believe in the Creed. By placing oneself in this midst, God becomes decentralized,

---

[19] The Settlers in Liberia are the Americo-Liberians and the recaptured persons who came out of slavery following the Atlantic Slave Trade. As the name implies, the Americo-Liberians came from the United States, under the auspices of the American Colonization Society, in the 1820.

and God is personal, and thus, God will hear the person in this manner.

Translation of materials of the church in Bassa was not just mission effort. Bassa men and women who were (are) literate in the language, were (are) willing to learn the English language to be able to translate the word of God to others. One thing that makes Bassa People unique among the other indigenous people is their ability to have their own writing system. But when translated, what does the Creed say to the Bassa People. What are they saying as they recite the Creed?

The version of the Creed used by Bassa people is the one that comes out of the Methodist Book of Worship, which is also an adoption of the liturgical style of the Church of England, of which John Wesley, Methodism's founder, was a clergyman. How did this version reach the Bassa People in Liberia?

The Meaning of the Creed as Recitation

The translation of the Creed to Bassa from English by the missionaries, assisted by locals, had one major objective: to fulfill the Gospel of Jesus to "all nations and in every tongue."[20] As Pelikan states, "helping to realize the eschatological vision prophesized by the seer of the apocalypse of every nation, all tribes and peoples and tongues," the translation of the Creed had this objective. Furthermore, and with specific reference to the Bassa Christians, this translation intended to make it easier to communicate the Gospel of Christ, or this eschatological vision.[21] The translation further helped to fulfill the functions of confessional, doxological, catechetical, kerygmatic, apologetic, and

---

[20] Jaroslav Pelikan, *Credo,* (2003), 306.
[21] Ibid.

integrative, with reference to the Gospel.[22] Each of these categories can be applied to the Creed among Bassa Christians.

Bassa people recite the Creed in their context. The presumption here for the context is that they do not read the Creed in isolation of other texts. For example, the Creed parallels the 23rd Psalm or the Lord's Prayer in that they are memorized. The translation of the Creed that we have is basically translation that makes the doctrine sound different from its original intent.

This is an example of what Stephen Bevans says. He observes in his *Models of Contextual Theology*, that "translation has to be idiomatic." If one considers Bevans' model, that "theology must be contextual" then the Apostles' Creed to Bassa people deserves a second look, and this second look must be in the context of Bassa culture.

This then brings us to the cultural aspect of the Apostles' Creed. In Bassa Christian culture, this is an important aspect of the liturgy, especially in mainline churches such as the Methodist, Catholic, and Episcopal churches. For most of these congregations which are indigenous Bassa language churches, the entire liturgy is translated in Bassa. Even hymns such as "What a Friend We Have in Jesus,' "Blessed Assurance," "Sweet Hour of Prayer," among others, if they are selected for that Sunday or that occasion, they are translated in Bassa.

The translation of the liturgy, including the Apostles' Creed is a cultural reality, but also an exercise in local theology. Schreiter observes that cultural patterns affect theological forms.[23] He says, "Not only is it a matter of how meaning is organized in a culture, but also how it

---

[22] Roland Modras. "The Functions and Limitations of Creedal Statements." *An Ecumenical Confession of Faith.* Hans Kung & Jurgen Moltmann (Eds.). (New York: The Seabury Press, 1979): 36-44.
[23] Robert Schreiter. *Constructing Local Theologies.* (Maryknoll, New York: Orbis Books, 1992), 31.

is communicated."[24] In the case of the Apostles' Creed, the Bassa cultural patterns do affect how the meaning of the creed comes out. The ideas are from the Bassa which, when listed for reading would mean something different than what is in the English version, as shown in the example below.

> *The truth of the Big God ... Jesus comes in the Big Spirit ... Virgin Mary's biological child; He suffered, he died in front of King Pilate ... That's where he is now, for our sake ... He will come again to plead on behalf of us (the world) ... I believe ... In the truth of God's Big Spirit, In the truth of those who talk or speak about God ... In the truth of forgiveness of sins.*

The idea of confession as affirmation of their faith in God, and in Jesus Christ, allows them to relate to God. In this collective fashion they see themselves as confessing a collective sin to God. Rather, they are expressing a confidence in a God that will guide them. In this context, the creed does function as a confessional tool because it calls the people to place God in their individual circumstances, with they believe, God hears.

The other category that Modras employs regarding creedal statements is that the statements are "doxological."[25] If one considers the word doxology in the context of hymns or liturgical formula ascribing the glory to God,[26] the creed, as recited by Bassa Christians, will fit the category of doxology. But since there is the Gloria Patria which Bassa Christians understand as the doxology, it will be farfetched to consider the creed in this context. The doxology[27] in Bassa usage is sung during the service at the appropriate liturgical moment, and although it has the Trinitarian idea, it is not considered the Apostles''

---

[24] Ibid.
[25] Modras, 37-38.
[26] Sidney Landau. (Ed.). *Chambers English Dictionary.* (Edinburgh: W. R. Chambers Ltd., 1990): 428.
[27] "Praise God from who all blessings flow/Praise Him all creatures here below/ Praise Him all earthly heavenly host/Praise Father, Son, and Holy Ghost."

Creed, and vice versa. This Trinitarian notion is the only parallel one can draw between the Creed and the Doxology among Bassa Christian liturgy.

Bassa Creedal liturgy usage is particularly restricted to a liturgical moment in the service, not in a catechetical framework. In the branches of the Roman Catholic Church, where there are Bassa members, this catechetical use, especially as a baptismal formula, is possible. However, in Bassa congregations, which do not exist among Catholics in Liberia up to this point, there is not a baptismal formula in most congregations, because in most of these congregations this formula comes in a separate outside the creed. Among Bassa Methodists,[28] for example, the Book of Worship provides liturgical blueprint for each of these activities, whether creed, baptism, acceptance of new members in the congregation, funeral service, or marriage. Each activity has a unique place in the church. Therefore, the Creed is not used for catechetical purposes, especially not in the sense of the Catholic usage of the idea.

Another function or understanding of the Creed among Bassa people is in is kerygmatic context, Modras' fourth function. The creed, among Bassa Christians, is kerygmatic because it functions, or it is understood, as a memorized version of the Christian message. In this message, God is not merely a heavenly father but an earthly father as well. While God is not a physical reality in their lives, as they recite, they "see" God as an Ancestor who functions in that light.

Furthermore, as the creedal recitation continues, there is an affirmation of the father and the son. Jesus Christ becomes a brother, a mediator, and an ancestor, but one who is a little less of an ancestor as God. In this context, Jesus is a closer relative, a brother who is with the Father God, and who can therefore be a functioning ancestor in

---

[28] This also includes United Methodists, African Methodists, African Methodist Episcopal Zion, and Christian Methodists. 1

his role as a mediator, on behalf of the living. The parallel with Modras' understanding is that the "Christian message is translated anew and the Bassa people formulate in both fidelity and creativity, not only in memory but also in imagination."[29]

[29] Modras, 39.

7

CONCLUSION

The Methodist Church in Africa

The Methodist Church in Africa started in Liberia in 1820, with the formal establishment of the Liberia Mission Conference. The church has produced some of Africa's staunchest leaders and it continues to be a force for Christianity in Africa. As an African, one can only observe the growth, challenges, and personalities of the Church on the continent. The interest in this project is not selfish. The goal is simply to provide a historical trajectory into United Methodism in Africa for those who are interested, including missionaries, indigenous Methodists in and outside of Africa, and other historians and scholars. This is not a complete history in that it does not capture every aspect of Methodism in Liberia. However, it lays some grounds for further discussion and research.

Beginning with history of Methodist Mission in Africa, starting with Liberia in 1820, the Bishops William Taylor, Joseph C. Hartzell, and Gilbert Haven, paved the way for more missionaries who could spread the Gospel of Jesus, but also prepare and train local leaders to take over, using the Methodist Book of Discipline. These were all Caucasian Missionary Bishops, but their efforts are not counted in the color of their skin, but the content of their character.

The next segment of the book looked at African Methodist leadership, something, and one could call indigenous leadership. This is the leadership provided by Methodist seminary graduates or those educated in various universities at home and abroad. Because this is a very exhaustive list, I used discretion in discussing some of these Methodist seminary graduates, and church leaders. I also discussed and analyzed Methodist Missionaries to Africa over the years. The theory here is one of institutionalized racism and Eurocentrism, in presenting the Gospel of Jesus to Africans. Today, this institutionalized racism and eurocentrism dominate the show of African Methodist dominance in Africa. My analysis considered Mircea Eliade's theoretical basis of the movement back to the cosmos, the cosmic ritual of African Methodism.

Another segment suggested ways the church can make a more significant impact in its context. I argued that the *Book of Discipline* must be written to be more contextual while maintaining its connectiveness. The church cannot claim to be connected, when the *Book of Discipline*, the Bible - the two books that bind us together as Methodists in the world, proclaiming the Gospel of Christ – are written only in the Western context, and in English, Spanish, Russian, or Chinese – not in any African native language, like Bassa, Kpelle, Kru, Grebo, Gola, Kissi, Mende, Mandingo, Mano, Krahn, or Kongor – (Liberian languages). The two books mentioned do not reflect the African's theological, spiritual, and realistic views. The fact that we all must function according to the *Book of Discipline*; shouldn't we ensure that everyone who joins the church knows the *Book of Discipline*?

Methodism in Africa has succeeded in its expansion and its mission. Beginning in Liberia, this denomination has made, and continues to make, numerous contributions to the communities where there are members of the church. *The Methodist Church in Africa since 1820,* tells the story of how Methodism reached Africa.[1] Books and articles about the Methodist Church in Africa are limited to their various locations.

For example, Bishop Willis J. King writes *the History of the Methodist Church in Liberia* (1947). This history touches on the church's work in Liberia, but not any other African country. Also, Dr. John Kurewa's *The Church in Mission* (1997), is a short history of the United Methodist Church in Zimbabwe. Although it notes that the Methodist church in Zimbabwe started with Bishop Hartzell, who was assigned to Monrovia, the book is specifically a history of the church in Zimbabwe. There may be other materials available about the Methodist Church in other African countries, and chances are they will focus on that Country or Conference specifically.

---

[1] This includes the Methodist Church, Methodist Episcopal Church, and the United Methodist Church. In Liberia also, this category fits the African Methodist Episcopal (AME) Church.

APPENDIX:
LIST OF METHODIST BISHOPS
WHO SERVED IN AFRICA

Name	Year Elected	Location
Francis Burns	1858	Monrovia
John Wright Roberts	1866	Monrovia
Gilbert Haven	1872	Monrovia
William Taylor	1884	Liberia/Congo
Joseph Crane Hartzell	1896	Liberia/Zimbabwe
Isaiah Benjamin Scott	1904	Liberia
Alexander Priestly Camphor	1916	Liberia
Eben S. Johnson	1916	Zimbabwe
Matthew Wesley Claire, Sr.	1920	Liberia
John McKendree Springer	1936	Zimbabwe/Congo
Newell Snow Booth	1944	Zimbabwe
Willis Jefferson King	1944	Liberia
Ralph Edward Dodge	1956	Zimbabwe
Prince Albert Taylor, Jr.	1956	Liberia
John Wesley Shungu	1964	Congo
Escrivao Anglaze Zunguze	1964	Mozambique
Stephen Trowen Nagbe	1965	Liberia

Abel Tendekayi Muzorewa	1968	Zimbabwe
Emilio J. M. de Carvalho	1972	Angola/West Angola
Fama Onema	1972	Central Congo
Bennie deQuency Warner	1973	Liberia
Moises Kainda Katembo	1980	South Congo
Arthur Flumo Kulah	1980	Liberia/Nigeria
Domingos Fernedes	1988	Angola/East Angola
Jao Somane Machado	1988	Mozambique
Done Peter Dabale	1992	Nigeria
Christopher Jokomo	1992	Zimbabwe
Ntambo Nkulu Ntanda	1996	North Katanga
Gaspar Jao Domingos	2000	Western Angola
John G. Innis, Sr.	2000	Liberia
Jose Quipungo	2000	Eastern Angola
Eben Nhiwatiwa	2004	Zimbabwe
Benjamin Boni	2005	Cote d'Ivoire
David Yemba	2005	Central Congo
Daniel A. Wandabula	2006	Zimbabwe
Kefas Kane Mavula	2007	Nigeria
Joaquiana Filipe Nhanala	2008	Mozambique
John K. Yambasu	2008	Sierra Leone
Mande Muyambo	2017	Congo
Gabriel Unda	2012	East Congo
John Wesley Yohannah	2012	Nigeria
Samuel Quire	2016	Liberia

BIBLIOGRAPHY

Achebe, Chinua. *Things Fall Apart*. New York: Fawcett Books, 1959.

Ahlstrom, Sydney. *A Religious History of the American People.* New Haven, Connecticut: Yale University Press, 1997.

Atlanta Daily World. "Miss Anna Hall Dies, Outstanding Citizen," *Atlanta Daily World*, Sunday, March 8, 1964.

Bevans, Stephen B. *Models of Contextual Theology*. Maryknoll, New York: Orbis Books, 1992.

Bogger, Tommy L. *Free Blacks in Norfolk: The Darker Side of Freedom,* Charlottesville, Virginia: University of Virginia Press, 1997.

Brown, Frank, et.al. (Eds). *Norfolk Remembers: Carrying Christ to Africa*, Richmond, Virginia, 1932.

Burrowes, Carl Patrick. "Black Christian Republicans: Delegates to the 1847 Liberia constitutional Convention", in *Liberian Studies Journal*, XIV, 2, 1989, 64-89.

Campbell, Barbara E. "Hartzell, Joseph Crane," in Yrigoyen, Charles & Susan E. Warrick (Eds.). *Historical Dictionary of Methodism.* Lanham, Md. & London: The Scarecrow Press, Inc., 1996.

Camphor, Alexander Priestley. *Missionary Story Sketches folklore from Africa*, The Black Heritage Library collection. Freeport, New York: Books for Libraries Press First published 1909, Reprinted 1971.

Cox, Gresham S. *Remains of Melville B. Cox, Late Missionary to Liberia*. New York: T. Mason and G. Lane, 1839.

Cox, J. Larmark. *Handbook for Conference, District, and Local Church Leaders: The Liberia Annual Conference, the United Methodist Church.* Lithonia, Georgia: SCP/Third World Literature Publishing House, 1994.

Davis, E. *The Bishop of Africa; or the Life of William Taylor,* DD [1885], Forgotten Books, 2018.

Early, Sr., Rev. J. Cephas. *Memoirs: the UMC among the Bassa People of Liberia.* Decatur, Georgia: Unpublished Manuscript, 1998.

Ericksson, Kare. *The Life of Bishop Hartzell: a Sketch of the Life and Work of Bishop Joseph Crane Hartzell, 1896-1916.* Umtali, Rhodesia Mission Publication, 1972.

Fadely, Anthony D. *God Power in Africa.* Cocoa, Florida: Fadely & Associates, 1983.

Fea, John. *Was America Founded as a Christian Nation? A Historical Introduction.* Louisville, Kentucky: Westminster/John Knox Press, 2011.

Franklin, D. Bruce. "The White Methodist Image of the American Negro Emigrant to Liberia, West Africa, 1833 – 1848. *Methodist History*, Vol. XV, # 3, (April 1997), 147–66.

"Funeral Service Bulletin of Ms. Anna E. Hall," *Central Methodist Church*, Atlanta, Georgia, March 1964.

Gravely, William. *Gilbert Haven: Methodist Abolitionist.* Nashville, Tennessee: Abingdon Press, 1973.

Greene, Graham. *Journey without Maps.* New York, New York: Penguin Books.

Hagan, Rev. William T. President; Rev. C. Alexander Lincoln, Secretary. *Official Journal of the Liberia Annual Conference,* held in Harper, Cape Palmas, February 11–17, Monrovia, Liberia: Methodist Mission Press, 1903.

Hartzell, Joseph C. *The Africa Mission of the Methodist Episcopal Church.* New York: The Board of Foreign Mission of the Methodist Episcopal Church

Hartzell, Joseph C., President; Rev. William T. Hagan, Secretary. *Official Journal of the Liberia Annual Conference,* held in Cape Palmas, February 8–16, 1899. Monrovia, Liberia: Press of the College of West Africa, 1899.

Harmon, Nolan. *The Encyclopedia of Methodism.* Nashville, Tennessee: Abingdon Press, 1968.

Heard, W. H. "A Parting Word," *AME Review,* Vol. XXV, #1, (July 1908), 68-69.

Henries, A. Doris Banks. *Liberia: History of the First African Republic.* London: Macmillan Publishers, 1960.

http://www.umc.org/who-we-are/history-of-the-united-methodist-church-in-africa.

Huffman, Alan. *Mississippi in Africa: the Saga of the Slaves of Prospect Hill Plantation & the Legacy in Liberia Today.* New York: Penguin Group, 2004.

Hunt, Susan. "Teaming with Tanzania." *https://www.awfumc.org/tanzania.*

The Independent, June 8, 1880.

Jacobs, Sylvia M. *The African Nexus: Black American Perspectives on the European Partitioning of Africa, 1880–1920.* Westport, Connecticut & London: Greenwood Press,

Kealing, H. T. "A General Conference Letter to Theophilus," *The AME Review,* Vol XXV, #1 (July 1908), 68-69.

King, Willis J. "*The Negro Membership of the (Former) Methodist Church in the (New) United Methodist Church*." 1964.

King, Willis J. *History of the Methodist Episcopal Church in Liberia,* Monrovia, Liberia, 1951.

Kirby, James E. *The Episcopacy in American Methodism.* Nashville, Tennessee: Kingswood Books, 2000.

Kulah, Arthur F. *Theological Education in Liberia: Problems and Opportunities.* Lithonia, Georgia: SCP/Third World Literature Publishing House, 1994.

Modras, Roland. "The Functions and Limitations of Creedal Statements, in *an Ecumenical Confession of Faith.* Hans Kung & Jurgen Moltmann (Eds.). New York: The Seabury Press, 1979): 36-44.

Nassau, Rev. R. H. *Historical Sketch of the Missions in Africa, under the care of the Board of Foreign Missions of the Presbyterian Church.* (Philadelphia: Woman's Foreign Missionary Society, n.d

Olson, James & Heather Olson Beal. *The Ethnic Dimension in American History* West Sussex, UK: Wiley-Blackman, 2010.

O'Malley, J. Steven. "Haven, Gilbert," in Yrigoyen, Charles & Susan E. Warrick (Eds.). *Historical Dictionary of Methodism.* Lanham, Md. & London: The Scarecrow Press, Inc., 1996: 105.

Park, Eunjin. *"White" Americans in "Black" Africa: Black and White American Methodist Missionaries in Liberia, 1820-1875.* New York & London: Routledge, 2001.

Pearce, Roy Harvey. *Savagism and Civilization: A Study of the Indian and the American Mind.* Los Angeles: University of California Press, 1988.

Pelikan, Jaroslav. *Credo: Historical and Theologian Guide to Creeds and Confessions of Faith in the Christian Tradition.* Yale University Press, 2003.

Rael, Patrick (Ed.). *African American Activism before the Civil War: the Freedom Struggle in the Antebellum North.* New York & London: Routledge, 2008).

Robeck, Jr., Cecil M. *The Azusa Street Mission & Revival: The Birth of the Global Pentecostal Movement.* Nashville, Tennessee: Thomas Nelson, Inc., 2006.

Scott, Isaiah Benjamin, President; Rev. Thomas J. King, Secretary. *Official Journal of the Liberia Annual Conference*, held at Lower Buchanan, Grand Bassa County, March 2-7, 1910.

Sanneh, Lamin. "Translatability in Islam and in Christianity in Africa." Blakely, et al., (Eds.) *Religion in Africa: Experience and Expression.* (Portsmouth: Heinemann Books, 1994), 23-45.

Schreiter, Robert. *Constructing Local Theologies.* (Maryknoll, New York: Orbis Books, 1992), 31.

Shank, David (Ed). *Ministry in Partnership with African Independent Churches.* Elkhart, Indiana: Mennonite Board of Missions, 1991.

Siegmann, William. *Ethnographic Survey of Southeastern Liberia: Report on the Bassa.* (Robertsport, Liberia: Tubman Center of African Culture, 1969), 7.

Smith-Eastman, Rev. Marie. "Report of the Delegation to the West Africa Central Conference, held with the Sierra Leone Annual Conference UMC, Moyomba, August 11-16, 1992," *Conference Journal of the 160th Session of the Liberia Annual Conference, UMC*, Monrovia, Liberia (July 5-11, 1993), 214.

Staudenraus, Philip J. *The African Colonization Movement, 1816-1865.* New York: Columbia University Press, 1961.

Strother, Emma. W. "Black Women in United Methodism," *General Board of Global Ministries*, n.d.

Taylor, William, President; James H. Deputie, Secretary. *Minutes of The Liberia Annual Conference*, Methodist Episcopal Church. Monrovia, January 18-24, 1893.

Thomas, James N. *Methodism's Racial Dilemma*. Nashville, Tennessee: Abingdon Press, 1994.

Wilmore, Gayraud. *Black Religion and Black Radicalism: An Interpretation of the Religious History of African Americans*. Maryknoll, New York: Orbis Books, 1998.

Wimberley, Ann Streaty. "Called to Witness, Called to Serve: African American Methodist Women in Liberian Missions, 1834-1934," *Methodist History*, 34:2, (1996), 67-77.

OTHER BOOKS FROM
PACEM IN TERRIS PRESS

AFRICANA STUDIES

DJUANKAYU
THE BASSA-AFRICAN CREATION STORY
A Postcolonial Practical Theology
Pianapue T. K. Early.

AFRICAN ENCOUNTER OF FAITH & CULTURE
*Ritual & Symbol for Young People
in Tiv Society of Central Nigeria*
Clement Terseer Iorliam, 2020

BOTTOM ELEPHANTS
*Catholic Sexual Ethics & Pastoral Practice in Africa:
The Challenge of Women Living within Patriarchy
& Threatened by HIV-Positive Husbands*
Daniel Ude Asue, 2014

HUMANITY'S AFRICAN ROOTS
Remembering the Ancestors' Wisdom
Joe Holland, 2012

CHRISITAN SOCIAL TEACHING STUDIES

SUMMARY & COMMENTARY FOR PACEM IN TERRIS
*The Famous Encyclical Letter
of Pope John XXIII on World Peace*
Joe Holland, 2020

CATHOLIC LABOR PRIESTS
*Five Giants in the United States Catholic Bishops Social Action Department
Volume I of US Labor Priests During the 20th Century*
Patrick Sullivan, 2014

CATHOLIC SOCIAL TEACHING & UNIONS
IN CATHOLIC PRIMARY & SECONDARY SCHOOLS
The Clash between Theory & Practice within the United States

Walter "Bob" Baker, 2014

PACEM IN TERRIS
Its Continuing Relevance for the Twenty-First Century
(Papers from the 50th Anniversary Conference at the United Nations)
Josef Klee & Francis Dubois, Editors, 2013

100 YEARS OF CATHOLIC SOCIAL TEACHING
DEFENDING WORKERS & THEIR UNIONS
Summaries & Commentaries for Five Landmark Papal Encyclicals
Joe Holland, 2012

THE "POISONED SPRING" OF ECONOMIC LIBERTARIANISM
Menger, Mises, Hayek, Rothbard: A Critique from
Catholic Social Teaching of the Austrian School of Economics
Pax Romana / Cmica-usa
Angus Sibley, 2011

BEYOND THE DEATH PENALTY
The Development in Catholic Social Teaching
Florida Council of Catholic Scholarship
D. Michael McCarron & Joe Holland, Editors, 2007

CHRISTIAN STUDIES

ROMAN CATHOLIC CLERICALISM
Three Historical Stages in the Legislation of a Non-Evangelical,
Now Dysfunctional, and Sometimes Pathological Institution
Joe Holland, 2018

CATHOLIC PRACTICAL THEOLOGY
A Genealogy of the Methodological Turn to Praxis,
Historical Reality, & the Preferential Option for the Poor
Bob Pennington, 2018

SAINT JOHN OF THE CROSS
His Prophetic Mysticism in the Historical Context
of Sixteenth-Century Spain
Cristóbal Serrán-Pagán y Fuentes, 2018

POSTMODERN ECOLOGICAL SPIRITUALITY
Catholic-Christian Hope for the Dawn of a Postmodern Ecological Civilization Rising
from within the Spiritual Dark Night of Modern Industrial Civilization
Joe Holland, 2017

JOURNEYS TO RENEWED CONSECRATION
Religious Life after Fifty Years of Vatican II
Emeka Obiezu, OSA & John Szura, OSA, Editors, 2017

THE CRUEL ELEVENTH-CENTURY IMPOSITION OF
WESTERN CLERICAL CELIBACY
A Monastic-Inspired Attack on Catholic Episcopal & Clerical Families
Joe Holland, 2017

PETER MAURIN'S
ECOLOGICAL LAY NEW MONASTICISM
*A Catholic Green Revolution Developing
Rural Ecovillages, Urban Houses of Hospitality,
& Eco-Universities for a New Civilization*
Joe Holland, 2015

GLOBAL GOVERNANCE & UNITED NATIONS STUDIES

SEEKING GLOBAL JUSTICE & PEACE
Catholic-Inspired NGOs at the United Nations
Emeka Obiezu, 2019

BRETTON WOODS INSTITUTIONS & NEOLIBERALISM
*Historical Critique of Policies, Structures, & Governance of the International Monetary Fund
& the World Bank, with Case Studies*
Mark Wolff, 2018

PROTECTION OF RELIGIOUS MINORITIES
*A Symposium Organized by Pax Romana at the United Nations
and the United Nations Alliance of Civilizations*
Dean Elizabeth F. Defeis & Peter F. O'Connor, Editors, 2015

PERSONAL WITNESS STORIES

"BETTER FOR BEING WITH YOU"
A Philosophy of Care
Sister Bernadette Kenny, MMM with Tauna Gulley, 2019

RUINED FOR LIFE
Post-Missionary Immersion, Reintegration, & Conversion
David Masters, 2019

PADRE MIGUEL
A Memoir of My Catholic Missionary Experience in Bolivia
amidst Postcolonial Transformation of Church and State
Michael J. Gillgannon, 2018

WORLD RELIGIONS, ECOLOGY, & COSMOLOGY STUDIES

A HIMALAYAN HOPE
AND A HIMALAYAN PROMISE
India's Spiritual Vision of the Origin, Journey,
& Destination of Earth's Environment & Humanity
Thomas Pliske, 2019

THE WHOLE STORY:
The Wedding of Science & Religion
Norman Carroll, 2018

LIGHT, TRUTH, & NATURE
Practical Reflections on Vedic Wisdom & Heart-Centered Meditation
In Seeking a Spiritual Basis for Nature, Science, Evolution, & Ourselves
Thomas Pliske, 2017

THOMAS BERRY IN ITALY
Reflections on Spirituality & Sustainability
Elisabeth M. Ferrero, Editor, 2016

SPIRITUAL PATHS TO
A GLOBAL & ECOLOGICAL CIVILIZATION
Reading the Signs of the Times with Buddhists, Christians, & Muslims
John Raymaker & Gerald Grudzen, with Joe Holland, 2013

THE NEW DIALOGUE OF CIVILIZATIONS
A Contribution from Pax Romana
International Catholic Movement for Intellectual & Cultural Affairs
Pax Romana / Cmica-usa
Roza Pati & Joe Holland, Editors, 2002

www.ingramcontent.com/pod-product-compliance
Lightning Source LLC
Chambersburg PA
CBHW032139040426
42449CB00005B/312